Unearthing Business Requirements

Elicitation Tools and Techniques

Unearthing Business Requirements

Elicitation Tools and Techniques

Rosemary Hossenlopp, PMP
Kathleen B. Hass, PMP

MANAGEMENTCONCEPTS

MANAGEMENTCONCEPTS
8230 Leesburg Pike, Suite 800
Vienna, VA 22182
703.790.9595
Fax: 703.790.1371
www.managementconcepts.com

Printed in the United States of America

Library of Congress Cataloging-in-Publication Data
Hossenlopp, Rosemary, 1958-
Unearthing business requirements : elicitation tools and techniques / Rosemary Hossenlopp, Kathleen Hass.
    p. cm. — (Business analysis essential library)
ISBN 978-1-56726-210-0
          1. Project management. 2. Business planning. 3. Strategic planning.
                    I. Hass, Kathleen B. II. Title.
HD69.P75H674 2008
658.4'01—dc22   2007021199

10   9   8   7   6   5   4   3   2   1

About the Authors

Rosemary Hossenlopp is president and principal consultant of Project Management Perspectives, LLC, the project and business results improvement resource. From initiating projects to implementing best practices, Ms. Hossenlopp has delivered improved business value. During her time at top Silicon Valley firms, including Apple Computer, Tandem, and Compaq, and in new product development consulting, she was a part of many generations of both consumer and commercial software and hardware introductions.

She is invited to speak at national conferences and has delivered the following presentations:

+ Accidental Project Manager

+ Plan for Project Success: Business Requirements Roadmap

+ What a Project Manager Really Needs to Know about Requirements

+ How to Talk to a Project Manager

+ Viewing Projects Strategically: Key Choices in Product Development

Ms. Hossenlopp delivers seminars on Thinking Your Vision and Creating Your Personal Business Plan to professionals and small business owners. She received her B.S. from Oregon State University and her M.B.A. from Santa Clara University in Santa Clara, California, and is a professional member of the Institute of Management Consultants USA. Ms. Hossenlopp is a Project Management Professional (PMP) and implemented the Tools and Techniques initiative of the Silicon Valley Chapter of Project Management Institute (PMI).

Kathleen B. Hass is the Project Management and Business Analysis Practice Leader for Management Concepts. Ms. Hass is a prominent presenter at industry conferences and is an author and lecturer in strategic project management and business analysis disciplines. Her expertise includes leading technology and software-intensive projects, building and leading strategic project teams, and conducting program management for large, complex engagements. Ms. Hass has more than 25 years of experience in project management and business analysis, including project portfolio management implementation, project office creation and management, business process reengineering, IT applications development and technology deployment, project management and business analysis training and mentoring, and requirements management. Ms. Hass has managed large, complex projects in the airline, telecommunications, retail, and manufacturing industries and in the U.S. federal government.

Ms. Hass' consulting experience includes engagements with multiple agencies within the federal government, such as USDA, USGS, NARA, and an agency within the intelligence community, as well as industry engagements at Colorado Springs Utilities, Toyota Financial Services, Toyota Motor Sales, the Salt Lake Organizing Committee for the 2002 Olympic Winter Games, Hilti US Inc.

Ms. Hass earned a B.A. in business administration with summa cum laude honors from Western Connecticut University.

Table of Contents

Preface xi

About This Book. xiii

Part I – Requirements Elicitation at a Glance

Chapter 1: Introduction to Elicitation 3

What Elicitation Is Not. 4

Terminology 6

When Is Elicitation Complete? 13

Part II – Planning Requirements Activities

Chapter 2: Build the Foundation 19

Assemble the Planning Team 19

Review of Preproject Business Analysis Information 20

Chapter 3: Assess Project Size, Complexity, and Risk 25

The Project Complexity Model 26

Scale Requirements Deliverables to the Project Profile 26

Chapter 4: Conduct a Stakeholder Analysis 31

Identify Project Stakeholders 33

Identify Each Stakeholder's Role 34

Assign Project Deliverables. 35

Identify Stakeholder Project Interest. 37

Identify Stakeholder Power and Influence 38

Revisit Stakeholder Analysis. 40

Produce a User Analysis 41

Chapter 5: Determine the Project Life Cycle 47

The Project Life Cycle 47

Variations in Project Life Cycles 51

Select the Appropriate Project Life Cycle 65

Tailor the Project Life Cycle 68

Determine the Solution Delivery Strategies 69

Project Life Cycle Training 70

Chapter 6: Plan Requirements Activities. 73

Planning Requirements Activities 73

Detailed Requirements Phase Plans 76

Summary-Level Requirements Plans for Design, Construction,
and Test Activities 81

Summary-Level Requirements Plans for Delivery of the
New/Changed Business Solution 82

Requirements Planning Considerations 83

The Requirements Management Plan 83

Part III – Elicitation in Practice

Chapter 7: Brainstorming 97

Types of Brainstorming 98

Rules for Brainstorming 98

Tailoring Brainstorm Sessions 100

**Chapter 8: Requirements Elicitation Workshops and
Discovery Sessions** 101

Resolving Requirement Conflicts 102

Formal Requirements Elicitation Workshops 104

Business Process Improvement Workshops 104

Agile Requirements Elicitation Workshops 105

Rapid Application Design Workshops 106

Joint Application Development Workshops 106

Rules for Elicitation Workshops 107

Tips for Successful Workshops 108

Tailoring Requirements Elicitation Workshops. 110

Chapter 9: Interviewing **111**

Requirements Elicitation Interview Types 112

Benefits of Requirements Elicitation Interviews 113

Tips for Successful Requirements Elicitation Interviews 113

Rules for Effective Requirements Elicitation Interviews. 115

Tailoring Requirements Elicitation Interviews. 118

Chapter 10: Surveys **119**

Types of Requirements Elicitation Surveys 120

Benefits of Requirements Elicitation Surveys .120

Rules for Effective Requirements Elicitation Surveys. 121

Tailoring Requirements Elicitation Surveys. 122

Chapter 11: Documentation Review **125**

Benefits of Documentation Reviews 125

Rules for Effective Requirements Documentation Reviews. 125

Tailoring Documentation Reviews 127

Chapter 12: Analyzing Interfaces **129**

Benefits of Interface Analysis 129

Types of Interface Analysis Meetings 129

Rules for Effective Interface Analysis. 130

Tailoring Interface Analysis. 131

Chapter 13: Eliciting Supplemental Requirements **133**

Benefits of Eliciting Supplemental Requirements 133

Rules for Effective Elicitation of Supplemental Requirements 134

Tailoring Supplemental Requirements 134

Summary **137**

Appendixes

Appendix A: Sample Business Requirements Document 143

Appendix B: Sample Business Requirements Document—
    Use Cases. 165

Appendix C: Sample Requirements Management Plan 189

Index. **207**

Preface

The Business Analysis Essential Library is a series of books that each cover a separate and distinct area of business analysis. The business analyst is the project member who ensures that there is a strong business focus for the projects that emerge as a result of the fierce, competitive nature and rapid rate of change of business today. Within both private industry and government agencies, the business analyst is becoming the central figure in leading major change initiatives. This library is designed to explain the emerging role of the business analyst and present contemporary business analysis practices (the what), supported by practical tools and techniques to enable the application of the practices (the how).

Current books in the series are:

+ *Professionalizing Business Analysis: Breaking the Cycle of Challenged Projects*

+ *The Business Analyst as Strategist: Translating Business Strategies into Valuable Solutions*

+ *Unearthing Business Requirements: Elicitation Tools and Techniques*

+ *Getting it Right: Business Requirement Analysis Tools and Techniques*

+ *The Art and Power of Facilitation: Running Powerful Meetings*

+ *From Analyst to Leader: Elevating the Role of the Business Analyst*

Check the Management Concepts website, www.managementconcepts.com/pubs, for updates to this series.

About This Book

The goal of this book is to present principles and practices for pragmatic, effective requirements elicitation. This book is not an academic discussion of requirements-gathering practices, but rather is designed to provide critical information about why and how to plan elicitation activities and conduct elicitation sessions to capture accurate, complete, and useable business requirements. To *elicit*, according to Merriam-Webster,[1] is *to draw out information or a response*. In projects, *requirements elicitation* is the process of gaining an understanding of the business problem or opportunity through interaction with the actual users and other key stakeholders.

The purpose of elicitation is to gain consensus on the business need across the business units involved in the change and clarify and document the requirements in such a way that actionable information is provided to the solution development team. Organizations are increasingly interested in contemporary, advanced requirements management practices because of:

+ **Continuing project failure.** As discussed in *Professionalizing Business Analysis: Breaking the Cycle of Challenged Projects*, another volume in this series, inadequate requirements can account for 60–70% of projects that fail to deliver on time, on cost, and/or with the scope originally promised. Many studies show that improved documentation, communication, and management of requirements leads to increased project success.

+ **Increasing use of outsourcing.** Developers may be thousands of miles away from the project team that is managing the requirements. The need for comprehensive, clear, paper-based documentation is accentuated when teams are not co-located.

+ **Expanding need for contractual documentation.** Requirements are a commitment for performance. Vendors want to understand the scope of work so that they can make an informed commitment to completing the project successfully.

+ **Increasing professionalism of the role of the business analyst.** Project-based organizations in all types of industries are recognizing the need for professional business analysis.

The purpose of this book is to present simple but powerful techniques to plan and manage the requirements elicitation process. The book is structured into the following sections:

+ **Part I: Introduction.** This part provides a quick overview of requirements elicitation and defines some key business analysis terms.

+ **Part II: Planning Requirements Activities.** This part discusses the need for the business analyst to work collaboratively with the project manager and other core team members to create plans that customize the elicitation activities to the unique needs of the project.

+ **Part III: Elicitation in Practice.** This part discusses the primary techniques used by the business analyst and discusses which methods to use for specific project types.

The business analyst makes use of powerful tools and techniques to determine the real business need as part of solving business problems and seizing new business opportunities. This book is specifically aimed at helping the business analyst acquire the knowledge, skills, and competencies needed to be successful in both applying the tools and acquiring the mindset needed to successfully gather business requirements.

In the past, it has been thought that requirements elicitation, documentation, validation, and management are the easy part of project work and that development of the solution is the most difficult part. However, it is becoming increasingly clear that the most elusive and challenging part of projects is *getting requirements right*. Applying the best practices presented in this book will result in:

- Building the requirements plan to ensure the business need is determined

- Scaling the requirements activities to the size, risk, and complexity of the project

- Clarifying project terms that cause confusion to stakeholders

- Selecting just the right amount of requirements activity for the project

- Using powerful elicitation techniques to improve the requirements gathering process

Although the business analyst is the primary person responsible for requirements gathering, many project stakeholders benefit from improved requirements elicitation, knowledge, and skills, including:

- Project managers, who schedule and manage requirements tasks

- New product and service developers and testers, who build business solutions to meet the requirements

- Sponsors, who validate that requirements are accurate and fund project efforts

+ Customers and users, who receive and operate the new business solutions

The requirements elicitation techniques that we discuss in this book apply in virtually all types of project environments and business change initiatives, including:

+ New business process development, including the development of supporting information technology (IT) systems

+ Business process and system enhancement

+ Infrastructure technology replacement

+ Business process improvement and reengineering

+ Organizational change management

Endnote

1. *Merriam-Webster Online Dictionary.* http://www.m-w.com/dictionary/elicit (accessed March 28, 2006).

Part I
Requirements Elicitation at a Glance

Requirements elicitation is the process of gathering business requirements for a new business solution. Requirements elicitation activities are designed to draw out, extract, or otherwise obtain requirements for a new or changed business solution from business experts. The new or changed business solution may be a manual business process and/or an IT-enabled business system. Before elicitation takes place, the need for the business solution has been identified during the enterprise analysis activities of the business solution life cycle and the initial requirements and scope of the project have been defined. Figure 1-1 depicts the business solution life cycle (BSLC), our common framework for discussion in this series. Refer to *The Business Analyst as Strategist: Translating Business Strategies into Valuable Solutions*, another volume in this series, for a detailed discussion of the activities that lead up to project selection and funding.

Chapter 1

Introduction to Elicitation

In This Chapter:

- What Elicitation Is Not

- Terminology of Business Analysis

- When Is Elicitation Complete?

Business requirements are elicited by conducting interviews, workshops, note-taking sessions and feedback loops, and quality reviews with various sources to capture business requirements, user and stakeholder expectations, and system constraints and assumptions. Typical elicitation techniques, which are discussed in detail in Part III of this book, include:

- **Workshop sessions.** Formal working sessions with users, business and technical subject matter experts, and project team members and led by a facilitator. The goal of workshop sessions is to gather as much information as possible from a diverse group of subject matter experts to begin to drive consensus on the functions and features of the solution.

- **Brainstorming.** A process that is used extensively in requirements workshops to generate creative and innovative ideas.

- **Interviewing.** Systematic attempt to collect information from a person or group of people in an informal or formal setting by asking scripted questions.

- **Surveys.** Administration of a written set of questions to multiple stakeholders to determine information on customers, work practices, and attitudes.

- **Documentation reviews.** The review of existing system, business policy, and contractual documentation.

- **Interfaces reviews.** The review of system, people, and process linkages external to the proposed business solution. System interfaces define system interactions—which systems provide input, which ones require output, and what medium is used.

Elicitation focuses on understanding what is really needed to allow the business objectives to be met by the sponsor or customer.

What Elicitation Is Not

The elicitation process occurs at the beginning of the requirements phase, as described in the business solution life cycle depicted in Figure 1-1, which is our common framework for developing new business solutions.

- Elicitation does not typically produce models—although it sometimes does.

- Elicitation does not specify the requirements attributes—although some attributes, such as requirement source and owner, may be identified during elicitation sessions.

- Elicitation does not deliver full documentation—it is only the beginning.

Figure 1-1—Business Solution Life Cycle

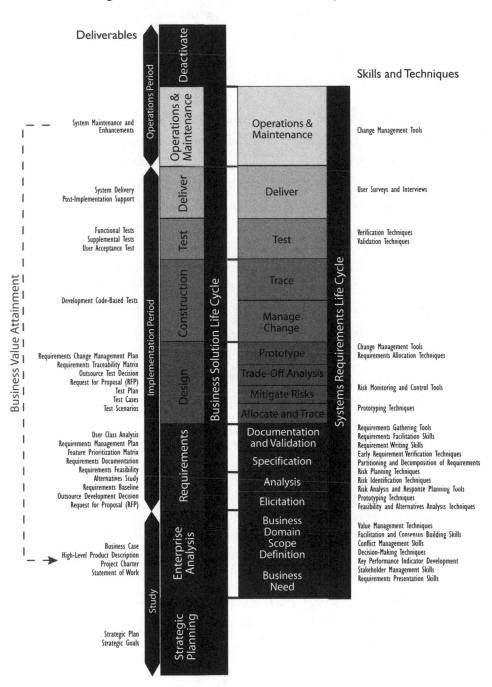

Business requirements expressly state the needs that a new/changed business solution must meet for the solution to successfully take advantage of a business opportunity or solve a business problem. Business requirements, then, are driven by and derived from the specific business value needed to achieve organizational goals. All too often, project teams begin by focusing on the solution before truly understanding the business requirement. Requirements elicitation activities are designed to give the project team an understanding of the business environment and to gather the customer and user needs that the project outcome is expected to satisfy. Good requirements elicitation practices provide the foundation to effectively analyze, specify, document, and validate the requirements.

> It is the business analyst's responsibility to transform business needs into a complete and actionable set of business requirements.

Terminology

Prior to discussing the processes for planning requirements activities and eliciting requirements, it is prudent to establish a common lexicon.

Business System

A *business system*, also referred to as a *business solution*, is comprised of all the elements that are necessary to make an organization operate, including: (1) business rules, policies, and procedures, (2) business processes that flow value through the organization to the customer, (3) organizational entities who own and operate the business system, (4) geographic locations of the organizational entities, (5) data that flows through the business processes, (6) application systems that support the operation of the business processes, and (7) technology infrastructure supporting the applications. The development of a new or reengineered business solution may involve changes to some or all of these business system components.

Requirements Types: Functional versus Supplemental

Business requirements are defined as those activities that must be performed to flow value through the organization to the customer. Business requirements are expressed first in terms of business objectives, and are then defined as a set of functional and nonfunctional requirements. *Functional requirements* define the behavior that is required within the business solution to deliver business value to the organization. Functional requirements are the features, services, tasks, and functions supported by the solution.

Functional requirements describe *what* needs to be performed, not *how* the solution will meet the requirements. As an example, a functional requirement may state that a user needs to withdraw cash from an ATM. The *what* is "withdraw cash." A functional requirement does not describe *how* the function will be provided in terms of hardware, software, and documentation components. Elements of the solution will be designed and constructed to support the functional requirement later in the project life cycle.

Nonfunctional, or *supplemental, requirements* provide additional information that imposes constraints that may modify the business solution behavior. They describe the appropriate levels of supportability, maintainability, security, or usability needed to satisfy a specific requirement. All too often, the nonfunctional requirements are overlooked early in the project. This often results in business systems that are costly to maintain and difficult to operate, thus eroding the business value of the solution.

When discussing requirements, it is helpful to clarify whether the requirement is a functional requirement or supplemental requirement. Table 1-1 shows the differences between these two types of requirements.

Table 1-1—Functional versus Supplemental Requirements

Functional Requirements Characteristics	Supplemental Requirements Characteristics
Are things the solution must do	Are things the solution must have
Describe user-required behavior	Constrain or modify the solution behavior
Are also called behavioral requirements and are often represented in "the solution or system shall" statements	Are also called nonfunctional, and often constrain the behavior of the functional requirement
Can be documented in text, graphical, or matrix formats	Can be in text or matrix formats
Are free from system specifications, constraints, or design assumptions	Constrain the solution design

In addition, it is helpful to use industry-wide conventions when describing requirements:

+ Business requirements use the word *must*. For example, "The accounts payable cycle time *must* decrease by 20% as measured from the preproject metrics." Note that business requirements cannot be coded.

+ Functional requirements use the word *shall*. For example, "The accounts payable system *shall* allow users to make modifications to the payment terms." Note that functional requirements can be coded.

+ Assumptions use the word *will*. For example, "Only internal users *will* use the accounts payable system during the first release." Note that assumptions cannot be coded, but add clarifying detail to functional requirements.

In addition to eliciting functional and nonfunctional requirements, the business analyst elicits information on *business rules*, which are the policies, guidelines, regulations, and procedures that govern how a system must respond to perform a function. As an example, in an insurance reimbursement system, business rules describe the formal criteria used to determine whether payments should be made for services and the level of reimbursement, depending on the insurance agreement.

These definitions are from the *PMI Combined Standards Glossary:*[1]

Assumptions: Assumptions are factors that, for planning purposes, are considered to be true, real, or certain without proof or demonstration.

Business Outcome: A financial result (cost saving, opportunity, employee reduction, revenue growth, revenue retention) derived from implementing an organization's strategies.

Constraint: The state, quality, or sense of being restricted to a given course of action or inaction.

Requirements *assumptions and constraints* are also documented by the business analyst.

Together the sum of requirements documents and models define the characteristics of the required solution, but do not say *how* the solution will implement those requirements.

Project versus Product Requirements

People tend to use the terms *requirements* and *scope* interchangeably. They are related, but they differ in important ways. *Project scope* is defined by *The PMBOK® Guide*[2] as the work that must be performed to deliver a product, service, or result with the specified features and functions. It is the sum total of the *work breakdown structure* (WBS) activities. A WBS is a graphically oriented representation of project scope. Activities are identified and organized hierarchically to show the sum of the project work to be performed.

When a WBS is used by a project team to identify the scope of the project, it effectively depicts the breadth and depth of the project work by presenting a deliverable-oriented grouping of activities. Senior management and customers can quickly review a WBS to see if the project team caught the vision for which the project was initiated. Corrections to scope in the early stages of the project are inexpensive, since the solution is not yet designed or constructed. Since project scope represents all the activities needed to plan, execute, control, and close a project, the project manager is responsible for managing the full scope of the project within quality, cost, and time constraints.

These definitions are from the *PMBOK® Guide* glossary:[3]

Product: An artifact that is produced, is quantifiable, and can be either an end item in itself or a component item.

Product Scope: The features and functions that characterize a product, service or results.

Project: A temporary endeavor undertaken to create a unique product, service or result.

Project Scope: The work that must be performed to deliver a product, service, or result with the specified features and functions.

Business analysts, on the other hand, are responsible for *product scope*, meaning the features and functions that will be included in the new business solution. *Product scope* is defined by the *PMBOK® Guide*[4] as the features and functions that characterize a product, service, or result. The *product scope* combined with the project management deliverables (e.g., project plans, reports, schedules) and solution development deliverables (e.g., design documents, test plans) together comprise the full project scope. Table 1-2 shows the difference between project scope and product scope.

The Business Requirements Document

The elicitation deliverables are the notes and various models developed during elicitation sessions and typically captured in an early draft of the *business requirements document* (BRD). The BRD con-

Table 1-2—Project versus Product Scope

	Project Scope	Product Scope
Lead Roles	Project manager	Business analyst
Deliverables	<ul><li>Project plans</li><li>Project monitoring and control</li><li>Project reporting</li><li>Replanning</li></ul>	<ul><li>Requirements management plan</li><li>Business requirements</li><li>User acceptance</li></ul>

tains the information that clarifies the *functions* of the solution for both the business and technical stakeholders. Ideally, organizations create a methodology providing a step-by-step approach to creating business requirements that are captured in a predefined BRD template (see Appendixes A and B for sample BRD templates). Customers review and validate the BRD to confirm that it accurately represents their needs, subsequently agreeing to fund solution design and construction. IT architects, design analysts, developers, and testers use the requirements documentation to begin their solution design and development activities. The requirements in the BRD are expressed in natural language to describe the needs, wants, and behavioral requirements of the solution. A BRD:

+ Translates business objectives and needs into requirements statements

+ States needs in a manner that is solution independent

+ Contains text, graphical, and matrix documentation

+ Conforms to enterprise standards

+ Is consistent with the product development methodology of the organization

+ Is sometimes referred to as a *product vision document*

A BRD is not:

+ A system specification, which comes later, in the design phase

+ A business case, which comes earlier, in the preproject enterprise analysis phase

+ A project plan, which is often created at the same time the requirements are being documented, because it is difficult, if not impossible, to prepare a complete project plan without an understanding of the requirements and a high-level concept of the solution that is to be constructed. Figure 1-2 depicts the two primary consumers of the BRD.

Statement of Work

The initial draft of the *statement of work* (SOW) is often first crafted by the business analyst during the elicitation process and finalized during requirements analysis, specification, and validation. The SOW is defined as a contractual document that outlines the expectations (requirements) of the customer and authorizes the performing organization to begin work. The SOW is often used as a component of a contract when the design and development of the solution is outsourced to a third party. There are several common issues with the SOW that the business analyst seeks to resolve:

Figure 1-2—Primary Consumers of the BRD

| Business Community | Business Requirements Document | Technical Development Team |

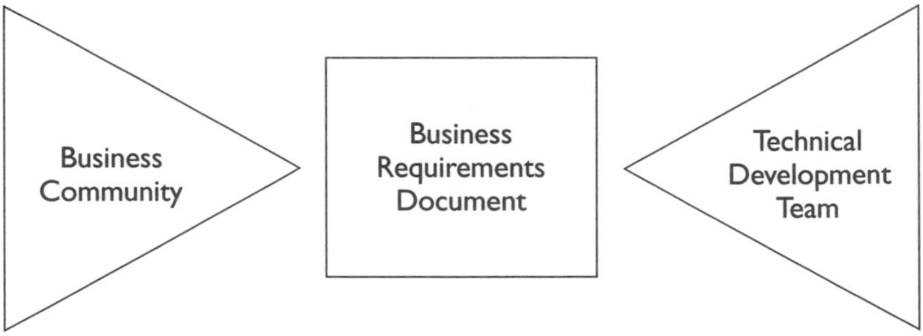

+ The requirements are often ambiguous, inaccurate, and incomplete.

+ The customer does not participate in reviews to validate and further define the requirements stated in the SOW.

+ The performing organization wants to begin immediate work against the SOW without validation of the requirements.

When Is Elicitation Complete?

At the conclusion of the elicitation activities, the business analyst leads efforts to review and refine the draft requirements statements and models before commencing the requirements analysis activities. The business analyst often conducts reviews with both the customer and technical subject matter experts to verify that the requirements are complete and ready for rigorous analysis. The reviews are designed to validate that the initial set of requirements are:

+ **Clear.** All stakeholders agree on what the requirements mean and terms are understood and documented.

+ **Consistent.** The requirements do not conflict with any other stated requirements or formal project documentation.

+ **Complete.** The breadth of the functions and features to be provided is fully understood and captured (the depth will be progressively elaborated during analysis, specification, and final documentation activities).

+ **Validated.** The requirements can be linked to an upstream customer or sponsor document that initiated the project; the business and technical teams have reviewed and approved the breadth of the requirements.

After requirements are elicited and initially documented, they drive all downstream analysis, design, development, and testing activities. Often, once a team of users, customers, and managers has drafted requirements, organizations expect development teams to immediately begin designing and developing the solution. However, requirements must still be analyzed, decomposed, documented in multiple forms, and further elaborated to ensure they are accurate, complete, and unambiguous before being released to downstream phases (refer to *Getting It Right: Business Requirement Analysis Tools and Techniques*, another volume in this series, for more information). During requirements elicitation, an iterative approach is recommended. Note taking and numerous feedback loops are performed often to determine if the requirements are fully understood.

Summary

+ Business requirements document the capabilities a new business solution must provide to achieve business objectives.

+ Functional requirements describe what a solution must do or how it must behave.

+ Supplemental requirements, also called nonfunctional requirements, are performance characteristics that the solution must have; supplemental requirements may constrain how the system behaves or modify how the user interacts with the system.

+ Requirements can be captured through text, graphically, or in matrixes.

+ Requirements describe *what* the solution must do, not *how* it will do it; in other words, requirements are solution independent.

+ The elicitation effort can be considered finished when the breadth of requirements is complete, consistent, correct, and unambiguous.

+ Requirements are accompanied by assumptions and constraints.

+ Project scope includes both the product and project deliverables to be provided by the project.

+ Product scope is defined as the solution components that are built to satisfy the features and functions outlined in the BRD.

+ The initial draft of requirements documentation is the outcome of the elicitation process.

+ The BRD summarizes the functional and supplemental requirements that must be satisfied to meet the business objectives.

+ A statement of work (SOW) is often used as a requirements document when outsourcing the design and/or development of the solution.

Action Plan for the Business Analyst

+ Separate the categories of requirements in requirements templates.

+ Include assumptions and constraints in requirements documents.

+ Have peers check to determine if the requirements are high quality and complete in breadth.

+ Create a defect checklist for all templates that lists common requirements errors.

+ Document all requirements-related terms, enterprise acronyms, and business domain language in an appendix to the requirements document or in a separate glossary.

Endnotes

1. Project Management Institute. *Combined Standards Glossary*, 2007. Newtown Square, PA: Project Management Institute, Inc.

2. Project Management Institute. *A Guide to the Project Management Body of Knowledge*, 3rd ed., 2004. Newtown Square, PA: Project Management Institute, Inc.

3. Ibid.

4. Ibid.

Part II

Planning Requirements Activities

Creating new products and services is the means by which organizations execute their strategies and remain competitive in the marketplace. The practices and techniques for capturing requirements for new or changed business solutions have traditionally received inadequate attention. As a result, planning the requirements activities is often considered to be a somewhat trivial matter and a standard approach has not yet emerged in the industry.

A new technique that is gaining popularity in the requirements management world is the creation of a *requirements management plan* (RMP). Since it is new, there is still a considerable amount of confusion about how to create an effective RMP. The RMP, which is the responsibility of the business analyst, specifies the requirements development and management activities and deliverables and is considered to be a subsidiary plan to the overall project management plan, which is the purview of the project manager. Prior to beginning the requirements elicitation process, the business analyst collaborates with the project manager, business representatives, and technical leads to create a plan for how to accomplish all requirements activities. The plan data are captured in the RMP. (See Appendix C for a sample RMP template.)

In this part of the book, we propose a step-by-step requirements planning process.

+ In Chapter 2 we provide an overview of the preproject business analysis activities that have taken place prior to approval and funding of the project. A review of this information provides the foundation to begin requirements planning activities.

+ In Chapter 3 we present a project complexity model that is useful for assessing project size, risk, and complexity as an important first step in the requirements planning process.

+ In Chapter 4 we present a step-by-step process for conducting a stakeholder analysis, followed by a user analysis.

+ In Chapter 5 we discuss the value of determining the project life cycle to be used prior to planning requirements activities.

+ In Chapter 6 we provide an overview of the requirements planning elements, including the resources required, activities completed, and deliverables created during the life of the project.

Chapter 2

Build the Foundation

In This Chapter:

- Assemble the Planning Team
- Review Preproject Business Analysis Information

Assemble the Planning Team

As the business analyst enters the requirements phase of the BSLC, the project manager is beginning to draft project plans. Although planning and conducting the requirements activities are the responsibility of the business analyst, they are ideally conducted in collaboration with a core team of experts and multiple groups of users and other stakeholders. The core requirements team typically consists of the business analyst, the project manager, one or more business representatives (one from each major business unit impacted by the project), and one or more technical leads (assuming the solution will have a significant IT component). Additional domain subject matter experts from the business or IT organizations are included as appropriate. The project manager typically takes the lead during the requirements planning sessions, relying extensively on the business analyst to heavily influence the emerging plans. Initial plans are drafted for conducting requirements elicitation, analysis, specification, and validation, and to begin to add detail to the solution concept.

Review of Preproject Business Analysis Information

Ideally, initial requirements definition has taken place in the early Enterprise Analysis phase of the project conception when the product description was created, and has been captured in initiating documents such as the business case, feasibility studies, and the project charter. All requirements should be traceable to these original sources. Figure 2-1 shows the ideal flow of information through the Enterprise Analysis Activities to requirements planning and elicitation. Refer to *The Business Analyst as Strategist: Translating Business Strategies into Valuable Solutions* for an in depth discussion of the Enterprise Analysis phase.

The first step in the planning process is to review all relevant documentation that exists about the project. For significant, strategic projects, it is almost always the case that a considerable amount of business analysis has taken place prior to the project's approval and funding. It is during the Enterprise Analysis phase that the initial requirements and scope of the project were defined and assumptions and time and cost constraints were documented. During the preproject enterprise analysis, some or all of these activities were conducted:

- Strategies and goals were analyzed.

- Current state business architecture was reviewed or built.

- Future state business architecture was built.

- Business problem to be solved and/or opportunity to be seized to achieve strategies were analyzed.

- Competitive analysis was conducted.

- Solution options were identified.

- Feasibility of each solution option was determined.

Figure 2-1—Enterprise Analysis Activities

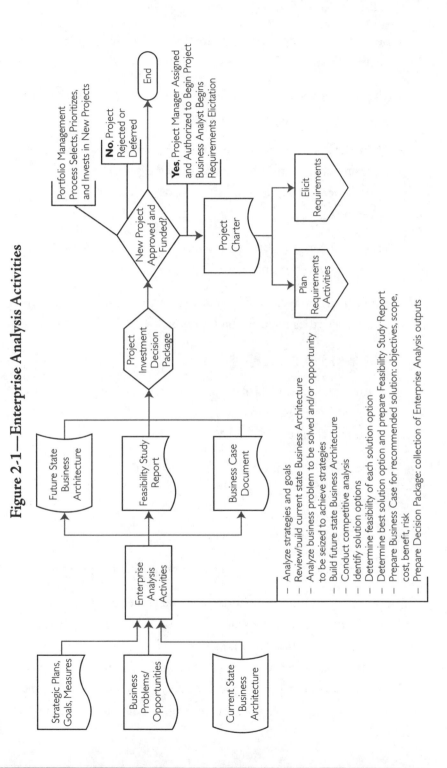

- Best solution option and feasibility study results were documented.

- The case for the recommended business solution—objectives, scope, cost, benefit, risk—was prepared.

- The investment decision package—a collection of enterprise analysis outputs and an executive briefing for presentation to management to decide whether to invest in the new opportunity—was prepared.

- The new project to build or acquire a new business solution was approved and funded.

Documents that may be available for review prior to planning the requirements activities include the following.

- Strategic plans, goals, measures

- Memos, papers, and other documents describing the current issues with business processes or practices and/or new business opportunities

- Current state business architecture artifacts

- Future state business architecture artifacts

- Feasibility study reports

- Business case and executive briefing proposing the new project

In some cases, an inadequate business analysis effort preceded the approval and funding of the project, and as a result there is little or no preproject information. If this is the situation, the core planning team should develop a minimum set of project documentation to be reviewed and approved by the project sponsor prior to continuing with the planning activities. Minimum project documentation likely includes:

- A project charter documenting:

  - The project objective

  - The project scope

  - Assumptions and constraints

  - The project sponsor

  - The project manager assigned

- A business case documenting:

  - Strategic alignment of the project

  - A high-level description of the business problem to be resolved and/or business opportunity to be realized

  - High-level business requirements

  - A description of the recommended solution, other options considered, and the rationale for the selected solution option

  - The organizational entities impacted by the project

  - The proposed project approach (make/buy)

  - The estimates of time and cost to build and/or acquire, deploy, and operate the new business solution

  - The tangible and intangible benefits the organization expects to realize after the solution is deployed

> Project challenges often start at the beginning of the project, when teams do not follow good requirements elicitation techniques. Teams often don't discover the problems until the end of the project, when the time and budget have been expended. At this point, additional investment in the project effort is likely to erode the business case, thereby negating the value the project was expected to deliver.

Summary

+ Preproject selection information is crucial to understanding the project objectives, scope, assumptions, constraints, and strategic alignment.

+ Planning is a collaborative endeavor, involving a small, core team of experts.

Action Plan for the Business Analyst

+ Assemble and educate a core requirements team composed of key business and technical stakeholders.

+ Gain an understanding of the needs and environments of customers, users, and stakeholders.

+ Review, or create if nonexistent, the business case, project charter, or similar scope definition document.

+ Understand the business vision, drivers, goals, and objectives for the new/changed system.

+ Understand and further document the scope of the project.

+ Define the documents and models to be produced and begin to develop the requirements management plan.

+ Define/refine the checklist of requirements activities, deliverables, and schedule.

+ Plan for change throughout the life cycle.

Chapter 3

Assess Project Size, Complexity, and Risk

In This Chapter:

- The Project Complexity Model
- Scale Requirements Deliverables to the Project Profile

The amount and type of requirements activities that are appropriate to each project vary depending on the size, risk, and complexity of the project. Opinions vary on how much upfront requirements development and definition is needed. Often, there is considerable pressure to rush through the requirements activities and have the solution development team begin design and construction as soon as possible. Using a defensible rationale to plan requirements activities will give you a powerful tool when asking management for the required resources and time commitment to produce high-quality requirements.

To objectively make the decision about which requirements activities to plan, and to determine the amount of rigor to use when eliciting requirements, it is helpful to analyze the complexity and risk of the project. Obviously, high-risk projects require heavier methodologies, tools, and techniques to reduce project risks. Small, rather straightforward projects need much lighter methods.

The Project Complexity Model

The Project Complexity Model shown in Table 3-1 can be used to determine the size, risk, and complexity of projects, and thus to determine the level of rigor required to manage the projects successfully.[1] It may be appropriate to update this model to make it more closely align to the complexities faced in the organization and on the particular project. Once the project profile is understood, the core project planning team determines the requirements activities and deliverables that are needed to manage each dimension of complexity.

To use the model to diagnose the size, complexity and risk of a particular project, shade the boxes that describe the project and apply the complexity formula described in Table 3-2—Project Complexity Formula.

Scale Requirements Deliverables to the Project Profile

The result of the analysis of project complexity, provides guidance for the project team in determining the requirements activities needed. This analysis also provides supporting information that can be used to present a rationale to the management team and/or project sponsor for the level of requirement elicitation and analysis rigor planned.

To ensure the complexity analysis supports project decisions, link the project profile to specific requirement deliverables to be created. Refer to Table 3-3 for a sample matrix of requirement deliverables mapped to project size, complexity, and risk. Note that additional criteria should also be taken into account when determining the requirements deliverables, e.g., organizational standards that the project must comply with or tools that are used in the organization to support the requirements processes.

Table 3-1—Project Complexity Model

Complexity Dimensions	Project Profile		
	Small Independent Low Risk	Medium Moderately Complex Some Risk	Large Highly Complex Significant Risk
Time / Cost	< 3 months < $250K	3–6 months $250K – $750K	> 6 months > $750K
Team Size	3–4 team members	5–10 team members	> 10 team members
Team Composition	Team staffed internally	Team is staffed with some internal and some external resources	Complex team structure, e.g., contractor teams, virtual teams, culturally diverse teams, outsourced teams
Competing Demands	Schedule, budget, and scope are flexible	Schedule, budget, scope can undergo minor variations, but deadlines are firm	Deadline is fixed and cannot be changed; schedule, budget, scope, quality have no room for flexibility
Problem / Solution Clarity	Easily understood problem and solution; solution is readily achievable using existing technologies	The problem is difficult to understand, the solution is unclear or difficult to achieve, or the technology is new to the organization	Both problem and solution are difficult to define or understand, solution is difficult to achieve, and solution likely to be using unproven or complex technologies
Stability of Requirements	Requirements understood, straightforward, and stable	Requirements understood, but are expected to change	Requirements are poorly understood and largely undefined
Strategic Importance Political Implications Multiple Stakeholders	No political implications	Some direct mission impact, minor political implications, 2–3 stakeholder groups	Affects core mission and has major political implications; visible at highest levels of the organization; multiple stakeholder groups with conflicting expectations
Level of Change	Impacts a single business unit	Impacts a number of business units	Large-scale organizational change that impacts enterprise, spans functional groups or agencies, shifts or transforms the organization

Table 3-2—Project Complexity Formula

Large Highly Complex Significant Risk	Medium Moderately Complex Some Risk	Small Independent Low Risk
Level of change = large-scale enterprise impacts OR Both problem and solution are difficult to define or understand, and the solution is difficult to achieve. Solution likely to be using unproven technologies OR Four or more categories in the "Large" column	Four or more categories in the "Medium" column OR One category in "Large" column and three or more in the "Medium" column	Remaining combinations

Summary

+ Use a defined process to determine the size, risk, and complexity of the project.

+ Plan requirements activities to be conducted and deliverables to be created based on the project size, risk, and complexity.

+ Consider other constraints, e.g., organizational standards and expectations.

Action Plan for the Business Analyst

+ Customize the project complexity model to the project environment.

+ Collaboratively determine the size/risk of the project and establish plans accordingly with the project manager and key business and technology experts.

Table 3-3—Sample Matrix of Requirement Deliverables Mapped to Project Complexity, Size, and Risk

Requirements Deliverables	Project Profile		
	Small Independent Low Risk	Medium Moderately Complex Some Risk	Large Highly Complex Significant Risk
Requirements Management Plan	Required	Required	Required
Business Requirements Document	Scaled-down version	More rigorous version	Full-scope version
Domain Model	Required	Required	Required
Process Models	Required	Required	Required
Proof of Concept Prototype	Not required	Required—paper prototyping methods acceptable	Required—paper and physical component prototypes required for all high-risk system components
Data Models	Required	Required	Required

Endnote

1. Kathleen B. Hass. "Living on the Edge: Managing Project Complexity." Originally published as part of 2007 PMI Global Congress Proceedings North America.

Chapter 4

Conduct a Stakeholder Analysis

In This Chapter:

- Identify Project Stakeholders
- Identify Each Stakeholder's Role
- Assign Project Deliverables
- Identify Stakeholder Project Interest
- Identify Stakeholder Power and Influence
- Revisit Stakeholder Analysis
- Produce a User Analysis

Stakeholders are persons and organizations such as customers, sponsors, direct and indirect users, providers, advisors, the performing organization, and the public that are actively involved in the project or whose interests may be positively or negatively affected by execution or completion of the project. A stakeholder may also be a person or organization that exerts influence over the project and its deliverables.[1] Project stakeholders are potentially sources of requirements.

The stakeholder identification and analysis process is designed to provide a common understanding among the core project team members regarding project stakeholders, their roles on the project, and their level of interest and influence on the project. The stakeholder list is then used, and often taken to a more detailed level, by the business analyst to determine the appropriate experts to participate in the requirements elicitation and validation activities. The stakeholder list, accompanied by descriptive information for each stakeholder, also provides guidance for communications during the elicitation process.

+ **Outbound from the project.** Information about the status of requirements elicitation activities is communicated to relevant stakeholder groups.

+ **Inbound into the project.** Information that is gathered during the elicitation activities is determined by the needs and level of influence of each stakeholder group.

A formal process should be used to determine stakeholder involvement. Tips for success:

+ Use team brainstorming to identify initial stakeholder categories or actual stakeholder names.

+ Focus on all stakeholders, not just the end-users of the solution.

+ Vague stakeholder definitions and vague needs represent risk to the project objectives and business solution adoption and should be identified and managed as project risks.

A five-step process for conducting a stakeholder analysis is presented in this chapter.

Definitions are from the *PMBOK Guide*® glossary:[2]

Stakeholder: Person or organization that is actively involved in the project, or whose interest may be positively or negatively affected by execution or completion of the project. A stakeholder may also exert influence over the project and its deliverables.

User: The person or organization that will use the project's product or service.

Identify Project Stakeholders

> Who Are the
> Stakeholders?

A complete stakeholder analysis can significantly increase the probability of securing accurate and complete requirements, especially if the following situations exist:

+ The project is critical and, therefore, quite visible.

+ The business solution is likely to significantly change user behavior and/or organizational processes.

+ The team expects management or stakeholder turnover, and therefore documentation of stakeholder positions is invaluable in ensuring new stakeholders maintain formal organizational commitments of their predecessors.

Stakeholder identification begins by listing all stakeholders that may be impacted by the project execution or the deployment of the new business solution. The project manager typically facilitates a brainstorming session (discussed in detail in Part III), involving the core project team to identify all potential stakeholders. The group uses the project charter and business case information to provide guidance to determine the organizations, groups, and individuals that will be impacted. This list needs to be further elaborated with the specific names of individuals representing stakeholder groups so the team can begin to communicate directly with appropriate personnel. Examples of stakeholder group representatives include:

+ A designated customer contact, who has the authority to commit resources and make decisions for the organization

+ A user champion for a specific business unit, who prioritizes requirements and coordinates user acceptance testing for that team

Identify Stakeholders' Roles

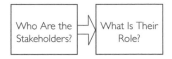

To document and clarify key stakeholder roles, a RACI (*responsible*, *accountable*, *consulted*, *informed*) model is a useful framework. Each stakeholder will have one of the following roles for specific project activities:

+ **Responsible:** The stakeholder performs the project work activities.

+ **Accountable:** The stakeholder is accountable to the sponsor or to the customer for the result of the work activities.

+ **Consulted:** The stakeholder is asked for opinions on objectives, assumptions, constraints, or methods of planning and developing products or process due to expertise or position in the organization.

+ **Informed:** The stakeholder is notified of the outcome of project decisions.

The roles interact as follows:

+ The *responsible* business analyst *consults* with the core project team or a subject matter expert to identity the requirements elicitation techniques to use on the project.

- The *responsible* business analyst works with the core team and the *accountable* project manager to make the decisions on how many elicitation techniques will be included for the different stakeholders.

- The *responsible* project manager then develops a budget and schedule for the elicitation activities.

- The *responsible* project manager then communicates the individuals needed to participate in elicitation sessions to *informed* managers.

Use the information provided in the stakeholder analysis to begin to understand if there are significant requirements elicitation risks due to an inability to involve the appropriate stakeholders. The stakeholder analysis will also help determine if too many stakeholders want to: (1) only be informed, i.e., there is low interest in the project, or (2) be consulted on all requirements, i.e., there are potentially conflicting requirements that must be resolved.

Assign Project Deliverables

A well-designed project will not only clarify key stakeholder roles but will define as much as possible how these stakeholders participate in specific activities. The RACI resource assignment matrix is a useful framework for identifying project stakeholder roles and responsibilities. Table 4-1 depicts a sample RACI responsibility assignment matrix.

Formally allocate time in the schedule for the core project team to conduct a complete stakeholder analysis and secure agreement from management that the individuals will be made available to the

Table 4-1—Sample RACI Responsibility Assignment Matrix

	Project Manager	Business Analyst	Technical Lead	Customer
Activity 1, e.g., Creating interview plan	R	A	C	C
Activity 2, e.g., Creating interview questions	R	A	C	C
Activity 3, e.g., Interviewing users	R	A	I	I
Activity 4, e.g., Documenting interview information	R	A	I	I

project when needed. Review the information captured in the stakeholder analysis with the stakeholders on the list to clarify roles and expectations. Through this process, the core team might discover that stakeholders have differing ideas about the project scope or the elicitation process; the planning team then explores disconnects and drives to consensus among different stakeholders on how to meet the project objectives. The goal is to resolve conflicts on the requirements activities, deliverables, and resource requirements early in the project, prior to beginning elicitation sessions.

Tips for success:

+ Ensure all elicitation activities have at least one stakeholder or stakeholder group participating.

+ Explore and reconcile differences in viewpoints if multiple groups believe they are the primary source of certain requirements.

+ Confirm the roles and activities assigned with all stakeholders.

+ Secure management approval and commitment to provide access to the stakeholders when needed.

Identify Stakeholder Interest

It is helpful for the business analyst to make it clear to the stakeholders that they have an important stake in the positive outcome of the project. Clarify the expected business value, e.g., cost reductions, revenue improvement, unique approaches for solution adoption, productivity enhancements, and end-to-end process improvements—whatever is predicted in the business case for the project.

The business analyst interviews key stakeholders to explain their role in requirements elicitation and to validate that project objectives are aligned with something that is perceived by them as important. When conducting initial interviews with stakeholders, ask open-ended questions to determine their level of interest in the project. Ask questions such as:

+ What are your project expectations?

+ Do the expectations align with the stated project objectives?

+ How does the organization benefit from the project implementation?

+ Which stakeholders are impacted by the project execution or implementation?

Once all stakeholders have been interviewed individually or in small groups, categorize their input. This allows the business analyst and the project manager to develop a preliminary prioritization mapping interest levels to stakeholders. There may be significant mismatches in the interest levels needed versus the reality. If so, the project should not proceed until conflicts are resolved. Table 4-2 shows typical interest areas for different stakeholders.

Table 4-2—Sample Interest Areas for Stakeholders

Stakeholder	Interests	Project Priority for 1st Release
Users	✦ Enhancement in business process functionality	1
Sponsor	✦ Improvement in perception of organizational responsiveness ✦ Quick strike technical delivery capabilities	2
Operations	✦ Reduction in costs associated with maintainability and supportability	3

Tips for success:

✦ Identify and prioritize each stakeholder's interest.

✦ Align interests to the project scope:

▫ If new expectations emerge through these early interviews, it may be necessary to expand the scope of the project or even refine the project objectives.

▫ Recognize which expectations cannot be satisfied by the project and provide escalation paths for resolution.

Identify Stakeholder Power and Influence

At this point, sufficient information is available to analyze the level of influence of the stakeholders. The business analyst works with the project manager to determine the stakeholders' capability to positively or negatively impact project success. This helps determine the communication and expectation management strategy for the project. This information can be used by the project manager and the business analysts as shown in Table 4-3, depicting the relationship between interest level and power to influence the project.

The information can also be visually mapped to provide a view of all significant project stakeholders, as shown in Figure 4-1. Individuals or groups are ranked to understand where to allocate time and resources to keep the stakeholder groups and individuals informed and involved. Requests should be answered from people in the high importance and high interest section of the graph first.

Tips for success:

+ Stakeholder power and influence is sensitive information and is not meant to be distributed outside the core project team.

+ Use this tool to identify additional stakeholders based on:

  □ Political power

  □ New user groups

+ Tailor both the communication medium and frequency to stakeholders:

  □ Face-to-face meetings versus e-mail reports

  □ Frequent communication to critical stakeholders

+ Balance competing demands (scope, time, and cost) in reaching project decisions by understanding the relative power as-

Table 4-3—Relationship between Interest Level and Power to Influence the Project

	Low Power	High Power
Low Interest	Keep informed—lowest priority group	Use for opinion dissemination—important group
High Interest	Empower if interests aligned with project—important group	Manage stakeholders—most critical group

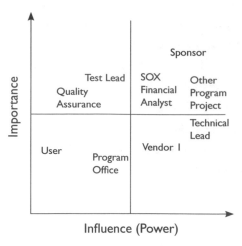

Figure 4-1—Project Stakeholder Map

sociated with the stakeholder groups. Some groups may be approached only as a courtesy, while others will be solicited for direct input into requirements.

Revisit Stakeholder Analysis

Reexamine the stakeholder analysis information often. It is likely that new stakeholder groups will surface as information emerges about the business area undergoing change. This iterative approach to the stakeholder analysis is illustrated by adding feedback loops to the process, as shown in Figure 4-2.

Figure 4-2—The Iterative Nature of the Stakeholder Analysis Process

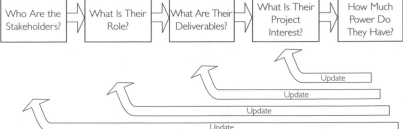

Tips for success:

+ Establish consistent communication checks and feedback loops with stakeholders.

+ Inform all stakeholders of current project decisions or enterprise environmental changes that impact the project requirements.

Produce a User Analysis

Business analysts complete a user analysis to identify the specific end-users impacted by the implementation of the new business solution. While stakeholder groups were identified as part of the stakeholder analysis effort, this activity decomposes stakeholder groups into user categories. Through the user analysis effort, all the different user groups and individuals are identified to ensure full participation in elicitation activities. The process is the same for any type of project or improvement initiative, and includes five steps.

1. Identify the End-Users

Using the stakeholder analysis information, identify all end-users who will be participating in the requirements elicitation sessions by name, department, and role.

2. Document Rationale for Participants

Documenting project justification as to why different sets of users are needed is essential before attempting to secure the resource commitment from the individuals' management team. Examples of rationales for the participants needed for requirements elicitation are as follows:

+ Companies that merge or even different divisions within a company have different processes.

- Individuals performing differing roles often require different processes.

- Roles require different security levels.

- Users have different expertise.

- Wealth, gender, or other characteristics that are relevant to the business solution must be taken into account.

- Users have different physical, cultural, and environment needs.

The user analysis attempts to identify the users of the new business solution and provides high-level assessments of how the solution should work *for each user category* to ensure that the requirements are accurate and complete. When planning elicitation activities, simply identify the users at this point and confirm with key project stakeholders that it is a complete and accurate list. It is not necessary to conduct a comprehensive user analysis to determine the unique needs of each user group at this point. Elaboration for user profiles, personas, or usability studies will be conducted as part of the analysis phase.

Each relevant user category requires an elicitation approach that must be incorporated into the RMP. If all the users are not included, adverse project results can be:

- Unusable systems

- Dissatisfied users

- Loss of public reputation

- Low usage by the intended users

- Missing requirements

- Project cost and schedule overruns caused by late discovery of requirements

3. Communicate to User Groups

Communicate the elicitation techniques that are planned activities to each user group. Examples of elicitation techniques by user group appear in Table 4-4.

4. Identify a User Champion

Identify a user champion who is authorized by the customer to speak for each user category and is available to participate in project elicitation activities. Although enlisting the help of a user champion is critical for projects using agile methods, it is important regardless of the project life cycle that is followed. The customer owns the requirements, and having a customer and/or business representative on the team and highly involved is an invaluable element of improved project outcomes.

5. Establish Ground Rules

Document the project guiding principles or ground rules relevant to categories of users. They state how decisions will be made. Examples of ground rules may include:

+ Allow for division or geography differences; this accommodates unique practices but is more expensive in terms of construction and maintainance.

Table 4-4—Examples of Elicitation Techniques by User Group

User Group Name	Elicitation Technique
Senior management, i.e., corporate	Interviews
Customers, i.e., lines of business or sales territories	Voice-of-the-customer surveys
Sales support, i.e., lines of business or sales territories	Facilitated workshops to develop use-case scenarios
Direct sales, i.e., lines of business or sales territories	Voice-of-the-business surveys

+ Document differences to provide effective training on new processes.

+ Requirements from one user group take priority over another.

Summary

+ Use a process for stakeholder analysis before beginning requirements elicitation.

+ A user analysis decomposes stakeholder groups in categories of users.

+ User groups have different requirements based on their role in operating the business system.

Action Plan for the Business Analyst

+ Bridge the gap between the project team and the stakeholders by establishing creative partnerships, conducting voice-of-the-business surveys, and securing customer input by establishing focus groups, business panels, and cross-functional decision teams.

+ Review the business case for a list of business drivers; continually link project work to the expected benefits outlined in the business case.

+ Explain the business value expected from the project to all stakeholders to continually confirm the primary needs that are driving the project.

+ Develop or refine the stakeholder analysis prior to beginning elicitation activities.

+ Use the stakeholder analysis to determine and manage early requirements-related risks.

+ Identify a champion for each user group.

+ Make the user champion a key member of the requirements elicitation team.

+ Establish and document ground rules for making requirements decisions and resolving conflicts.

Endnotes

1. Project Management Institute. *A Guide to the Project Management Body of Knowledge*, 3rd ed., 2004. Newtown Square, PA: Project Management Institute, Inc.

2. Ibid.

Chapter 5

Determine the Project Life Cycle

In This Chapter:

- The Project Life Cycle

- Variations in Project Life Cycles

- Select the Appropriate Project Life Cycle

- Tailor the Project Life Cycle

- Determine the Solution Delivery Strategies

- Project Life Cycle Training

Prior to planning the requirements activities, the core planning team needs to determine the development approach by selecting the *project life cycle* that will be followed. This is necessary because the requirements activities, their sequence and timing, and the requirements deliverables to be produced differ based on the project life cycle that is used. It is important to understand that whatever project life cycle is selected will impose some constraints that must be taken into account when planning requirements activities.

The Project Life Cycle

Project life cycles are used to add structure and control points to projects. Project life cycles attempt to bring order to project activities, thus providing a repeatable, predictable way to develop products. The project life cycle, usually depicted in a graphical model, acts as the framework guiding the project team through the project. It is therefore essential that the project life cycle is determined and agreed upon in the beginning of a project, prior to the start of requirements activities, since it defines what will be done from start to finish. The project life cycle identifies the technical work that is needed, the roles needed in each phase, and the control gate entry and exit criteria. A complete project life cycle defines the work from project management, business analysis, and IT perspectives:

+ Project management: The approach used to manage and control the project

+ Business analysis: The approach used to gather and document business requirements for the solution and to build, maintain, and retire components of the solution that are not automated by IT components

+ IT: The approach used to design, build, maintain, and retire the IT components of the solution

The *project life cycle* is combined with the *product* (or *solution development*) *life cycle* to create an *integrated project life cycle*. Figure 5-1 shows the *integrated project life cycle*.

Figure 5-1—Integrated Project Life Cycle

Project Life Cycle	Initiate	Plan	Execute Monitor Control	Close

Product Life Cycle	Requirements	Design	Construct Test Verify	Deliver	Operations Maintenance	Deactivate

These definitions are from the *PMBOK® Guide* glossary:[1]

Product Life Cycle: A collection of generally sequential, non-overlapping product phases whose name and number are determined by the manufacturing and control needs of the organization. Generally, a *project life cycle* is contained within one or more product life cycles.

Project Life Cycle: A collection of generally sequential project phases whose name and number are determined by the control needs of the organization or organizations involved in the project. A life cycle can be documented with a methodology.

Methodology: A system of practices, techniques, procedures, and rules used by those who work in a discipline.

The Iterative Nature of Project Life Cycles

Although the activities in project life cycles appear to be sequential, it is important to keep in mind that they are almost always performed iteratively. Iteration is an effective technique when attempting to control a risky process such as business requirements definition or business solution development. Candid feedback mechanisms should be planned after each iteration to uncover defects and apply corrections as early in the project life cycle as possible.

The key to allowing for continuous feedback is for the business analyst to plan an iterative approach to requirements generation throughout the requirements phase, and indeed, throughout the remaining phases of the project. During the requirements phase, the technical leads are likely working on early iterations of the solution design and perhaps even building prototypes of high-risk solution components. As the business analyst conducts requirements tradeoff analyses to determine the best requirement to achieve business objectives, the architect does the same for solution options. Thus, early prototyping is the first step in iterative development.

Industry- or Product-Specific Project Life Cycles

Organizations use different project life cycles, each containing product and project management activities, depending on the nature of the end product they are creating.

Construction Project Life Cycle

A typical construction project life cycle contains the periods and phases depicted in Figure 5-2. The three periods within the cycle are:

+ Planning: The period determining the project scope and direction

+ Design: The period designing the building, selecting the contractors, and securing approval from the buyer to begin construction

+ Construction: The period preparing the site, constructing the building, and preparing for turnover for building occupancy and operations and maintenance

Government Acquisition Project Life Cycle

A typical government acquisition project life cycle contains the periods and phases depicted in Figure 5-3. The three periods within the cycle are:

+ Study: The period determining the project scope, requirements, design, and direction

+ Acquisition: The period selecting the contractor(s) and producing and delivering the solution to the buyer

+ Operations: The period deploying, operating, maintaining, and deactivating the system

Variations in Project Life Cycles

There are many variations in business system development project life cycles. Most of these come from the software engineering world and the IT domain as the result of trying to reduce software development project risks. For most business solution development projects with a significant IT component, and even for many non-technical projects, at least one of these project life cycles will likely

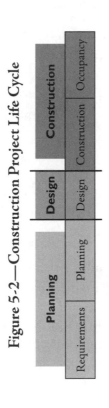

Figure 5-2—Construction Project Life Cycle

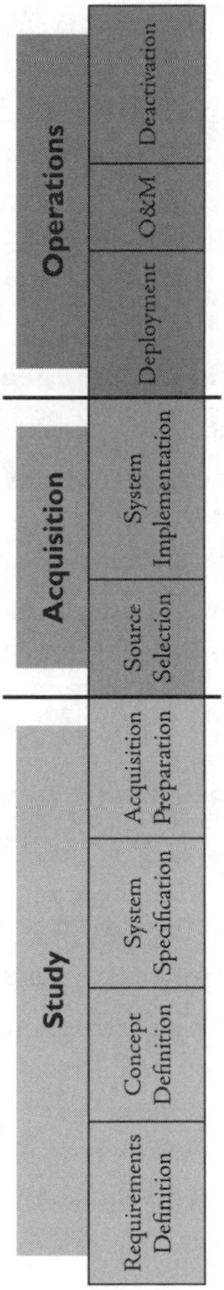

Figure 5-3—Typical Project Life Cycle for a Major Acquisition

meet the project needs. Given certain project conditions, each of these approaches has the potential to work well:

+ **Waterfall model**—Linear sequential development through the typical project phases: requirements, design, construction, test, deliver, operations and maintenance, retire.

+ **Rapid application development (RAD) model**—Builds system components concurrently and integrates the components at the end; used to compress the schedule.

+ **Vee model**—Includes the relationship between decomposition and integration, and the concept of incremental delivery.

+ **Evolutionary development model**—Build something and try it; learn from first cycle and try again.

+ **Spiral development model**—Risk-driven; develops requirements and system concept concurrently. Essentially an iterative waterfall model.

+ **Agile development model**—Risk-driven; risk is contained through the use of short development cycles and co-located teams. Used when requirements are difficult to define and expected to change.

+ **Legacy maintenance model**—Builds upgrades to existing systems; this abbreviated waterfall model is typically used.

+ **Prototyping model**—Builds nonworking mockups of the system or components of the system for proof of concept for high-risk areas or for requirements understanding.

Waterfall Model

The waterfall model is the classic solution development project life cycle. It is the oldest paradigm for software engineering, but it is also widely used as a generic model for other types of engineering endeavors. It is essentially a linear ordering of activities. The waterfall technique is rarely successful for large projects because users are typically excluded from influencing the product during development and must accept what is delivered. It presumes that requirements are fully developed and agreed upon and are very clear before the project moves to design and construction. It also assumes that events affecting the project are predictable, tools and activities are well-understood, and as a rule, that once a phase is complete it is not revisited.

The strengths of this approach are that it lays out the steps for solution development and stresses the importance of requirements. The limitations are that projects rarely follow the sequential flow. In addition, it is often difficult for the client to state all requirements early on in the project completely and succinctly, as required by this model.

The waterfall model endorses an "over the wall" approach, wherein responsibility for building the product is incrementally moved from one group to another. The contemporary movement, by contrast, is toward teams of people working on a *complete* project. The waterfall approach excludes an incremental approach to product development, which is probably much more realistic for complex projects. However, the waterfall model of project life cycles is highly effective for short-duration, well-understood projects with stable requirements. Figure 5-4 depicts the waterfall model.

Used When

The waterfall model is most effective for projects that are small, straightforward, predictable, independent, and low-risk.

Implications for Planning the Requirements Activities

When planning requirements activities, build the schedule to complete all requirements elicitation, analysis, specification, documentation, and validation activities in full prior to exiting the requirements

Figure 5-4—Waterfall Model

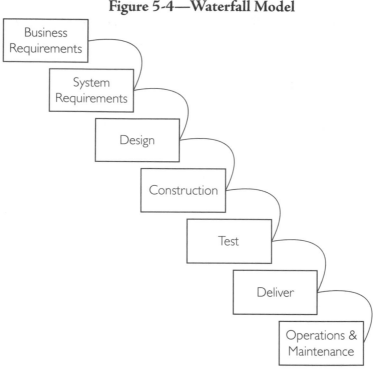

phase. Also, plan to baseline the requirements and implement a rigorous change control process.

Rapid Application Development Model

If requirements are understood and scope is contained, rapid application development (RAD) allows the system to be developed in the shortest amount of time. Also called *multiple build,* RAD is similar to incremental development with the exception that functional pieces of the system are being delivered to the customer. These pieces may stand alone to be integrated during a later build, or they may be an integrated set of partial functionality that contains an increasing number of features with each build. Previously delivered builds are usually not maintained in the field, since subsequent builds often require changes to them. Because this life cycle requires customer input into the total number of builds, the functionality within each build, and expected delivery of each build, the requirements and design phases are usually completed prior to developing, testing, and delivering various builds.

- Strengths: Greatly abbreviated development timeline; component-based approach allows for incremental testing and defect repair; and significantly reduced risk compared to single, comprehensive delivery.

- Limitations: Can be costly if requirements aren't well-defined (high risk of requirement defects) or the design is not sound (high risk of integration issues). In addition, many solutions cannot be structured into divisible subcomponents that can be worked on concurrently. RAD is highly effective for decomposing the development of a large, high-risk system into the development of a succession of smaller, lower risk subsystems. Figure 5-5 depicts the RAD model.

Used When

The RAD model is used most effectively when requirements are understood, scope is contained, and time-to-market is the most significant driver.

Implications for Planning the Requirements Activities

When planning a RAD project, schedule all requirements and design activities to be completed in full prior to beginning development of solution components. When the solution is developed through RAD techniques, it is prudent to divide the development of the solution into a *core system* (the operative part of the system), and *special components* (separate from the core, adding functionality in components). Further divide the core system into *extension levels*, building the foundation level first and then extending system capabilities incrementally. As the core system is developed and imple-

Figure 5-5—Rapid Application Development

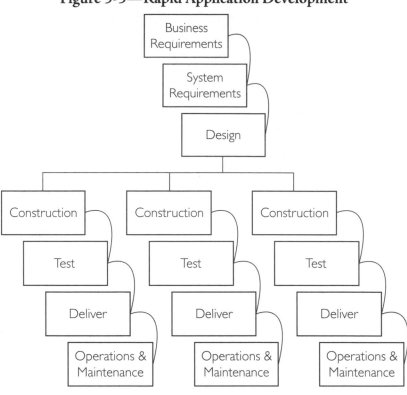

mented, different technical teams work on specialized functional components. The goal is to build the specialized components with only a one-way dependency to the core system; therefore, specialized components are independent of each other and can be created in any order or even in parallel.[2]

Vee Model

The vee model, which was created by NASA to manage project complexity, is often used for moderate- to high-risk projects. It includes the relationship between decomposition and integration, and the concept of incremental delivery. The vee model involves progressively elaborating requirements (the left side of the vee), while defining the approach to integration, verification, and validation (the right side of the vee) at every decomposition level. It assumes the requirements and testing processes, elicited through various business analysis techniques, are known before building begins. Figure 5-6 depicts the vee model.

Used When

The vee model is used most effectively when projects are complex, requirements are extensive and difficult to define, and a sequentially phased development process can be used. Note that when requirements are elusive, it is prudent to draft test cases first or concurrently with the requirements documentation. Drafting a test case can often clarify requirements and also ensures that the requirements are testable.

Figure 5-6—Vee Model

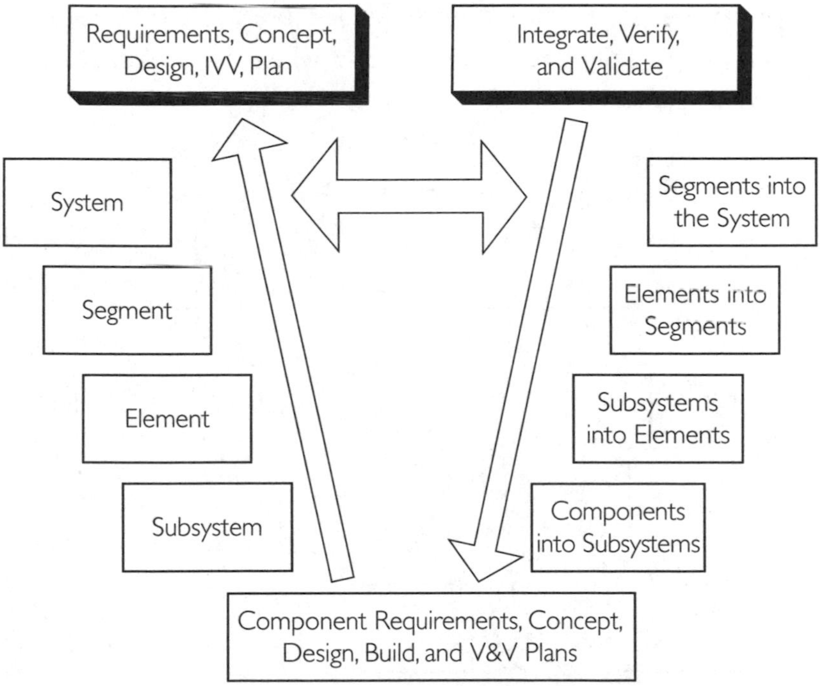

Implications for Planning the Requirements Activities

Since the vee model involves progressively elaborating requirements while defining the approach to integration, verification, and validation (IV&V) at every decomposition level, the requirements activities are scheduled in concert with the IV&V activities. Therefore, the requirements activities will likely be longer in duration, and will take place before building begins.

Evolutionary Delivery Model

Evolutionary delivery allows for building a simple, working version of the solution and then adding functionality incrementally to improve the product based on experience from prior versions. In practice, evolutionary delivery transforms a single vee into a series of vees. Figure 5-7 shows the typical approach to evolutionary development.

Used When

The evolutionary delivery model is best used when the requirements are not fully known initially and when the project is large, high-risk, and complex.

Figure 5-7—Evolutionary Delivery Model

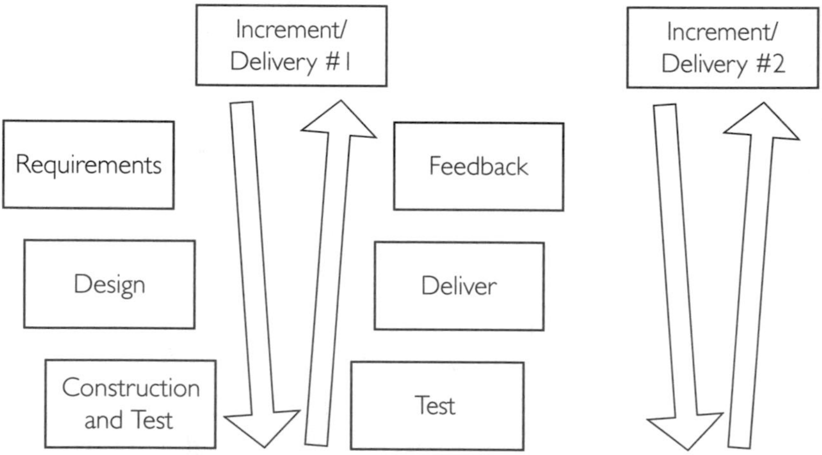

Implications for Planning the Requirements Activities

When planning requirements activities, each increment will include activities to elicit, analyze, specify, and validate requirements. Therefore, the planning effort involves scheduling the full life cycle for each increment, not just the requirements activities. Obviously, not all increments can be planned in the beginning; some can be planned only when more is learned about the solution requirements from early deliveries of simple versions of the solution.

Spiral Development Model

The spiral development model couples the iterative nature of prototyping with the controlled and systematic aspects of the linear sequential waterfall model. Using the spiral development model, the team keeps cycling through the same set of life cycle phases until the product development is complete. Each cycle is characterized by four phases: plan/requirements, design, build, and evaluate. Detailed plans are built only for the current phase of the spiral. Benefits include:

+ The development environment is tightly controlled.

+ Validation occurs early (good for large-scale systems and software).

+ Risks are addressed at each level, so risk is reduced.

+ The systematic, stepwise approach of the classic waterfall model project life cycle is maintained, but reframed into an iterative framework.

Used When

The spiral development model is very effective when the customer (or management) does not know what the final product should look like and a prototype will not answer the question. The purpose of each cycle is to attempt to develop whatever part of the system currently presents the highest risk (risk-driven spiral). The spiral model is used when it is important to test the reaction of the real customer using initial functionality before deciding what additional functionality would increase value. Figure 5-8 shows the complexity of spiral development.

Implications for Planning the Requirements Activities

When planning requirements activities, detailed plans (plan/requirements, design, build, and evaluate) are built only for the current phase of the spiral.

Agile Development Model

Interest has blossomed in agile development in the past two years, although the roots of the movement go back to the early 1990s.

Figure 5-8—Spiral Development Model

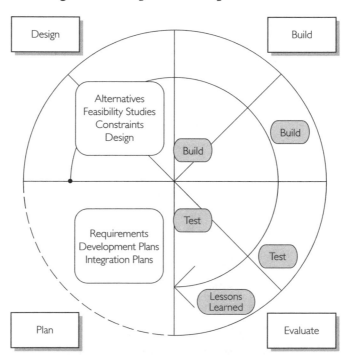

Agile managers understand that demanding certainty in the face of uncertainty (as in the waterfall model) may be unrealistic. The agile approaches focus on collaborative values and principles with a high degree of interaction among project team members and customers. Agile project managers rely on face-to-face interaction more than on documentation; they seek to avoid bureaucracy.

Using agile development, a project's overall scope, objectives, constraints, clients, risks, etc., are briefly documented, followed by short, iterative, feature-driven, time-boxed cycles. Using multiple exploratory cycles allows for constant feedback to stay on track. The focus is on delivering business value incrementally, which requires continued interaction between developers and customers. (For more information about agile development, see www.agilealliance.com.) See Figure 5-9 for a depiction of agile development.

Figure 5-9—Agile Development Model

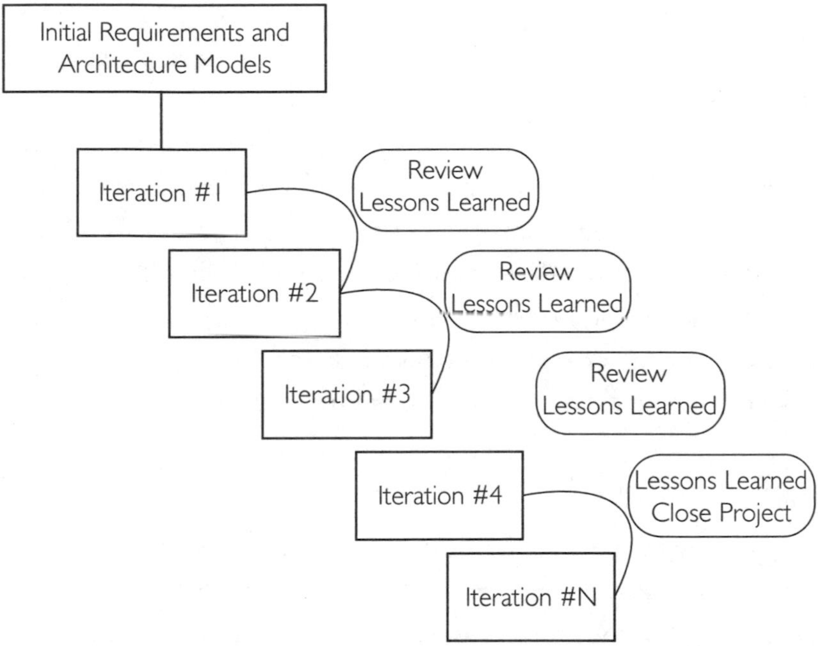

Used When

Use agile methods when these conditions are present: project value is clear; the customer can participate throughout the project; customer, designers, and developers are co-located; incremental feature-driven development is possible; and visual documentation (cards on the wall vs. formal documentation) is acceptable.

Implications for Planning the Requirements Activities

Planning a project using the agile development model is challenging. The business analyst works collaboratively with the project manager, the business representative, and the development team to plan the activities and document the scope, objectives, constraints, clients, and risks. In addition, the requirements and solution architecture are defined at a very high level so that a release plan can be developed for incremental delivery of the solution. After risks have been resolved, features delivered by each increment are prioritized based on business value.

The business analysis plans focus on building initial requirements models, prioritizing customer requests, validating increments as they are built and tested, reprioritizing the features in backlog after each increment is delivered, and reviewing the business case after each incremental delivery to ensure the project is continuing to add more value than it is costing the organization. Caution: While the agile development model focuses more on building models and code versus documents, the business analyst's challenge is to document the business and system requirements in enough detail so that the system can be maintained once it is in operations.

Legacy Maintenance Model

Legacy maintenance differs from new solution development in that it is usually a succession of parallel microprojects that involve fixing defects and implementing relatively minor enhancements to a solution that is in operation. Legacy maintenance can be thought of as one cycle: implement the change request. Maintenance teams usually follow an abbreviated waterfall model approach, which is generally successful, assuming the projects are small, well-understood, and low-risk. Figure 5-10 depicts a typical legacy maintenance project life cycle.

Used When

The legacy maintenance model is used most effectively for projects that are very small upgrades or fixes to existing business solutions.

Implications for Planning the Requirements Activities

The plan includes activities that involve tracking the backlog of work, working with a change control group to evaluate and prioritize changes, working with the maintenance team, and working with configuration management staff to ensure that fixes are not accidentally overwritten and that older versions of subcomponents are not reintroduced into the production system.

Prototyping Model

Prototyping often begins during requirements elicitation to confirm understanding of the requirements. The overall objectives

Figure 5-10—Legacy Maintenance Model

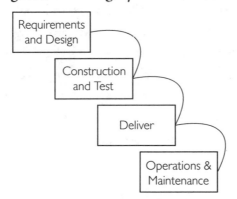

for the new solution that are known are defined, and areas where further definition is needed are identified for exploration through prototyping. For areas of risk, a prototype if often constructed to help visualize the solution. The prototype is evaluated by the customer/user and is used to refine requirements for the solution to be developed. Iteration occurs as the prototype is fine-tuned to satisfy the needs of the customer while enabling the solution developers to better understand what needs to be built.

Once complete, the prototype is used as a reference for requirements documentation, or it can be baselined and used as part of the requirements specification. There are two types of prototypes: (1) rapid prototypes, where the prototype is discarded, and (2) evolutionary prototypes, where the mockup evolves into the end product. Strengths of rapid prototyping are that it allows a small-scale trial in light of uncertain requirements, and it provides insight so requirements can be clearly defined and understood.

Used When

The prototype model is highly effective when requirements are vague, highly uncertain, or subject to volatility. Use when it is necessary to build something before requirements can be understood.

Implications for Planning the Requirements Activities

When planning requirements activities, consider building paper-based or physical prototypes while eliciting and analyzing requirements. To plan, begin with requirements gathering sessions and build a quick design. The customer reviews the design and refines requirements, and then the developers produce successive iterations as the prototype is fine-tuned to satisfy the needs of the customer. Figure 5-11 depicts the iterative nature of refining the prototype until is adequately fulfills the requirement.

Figure 5-11—Prototyping Model

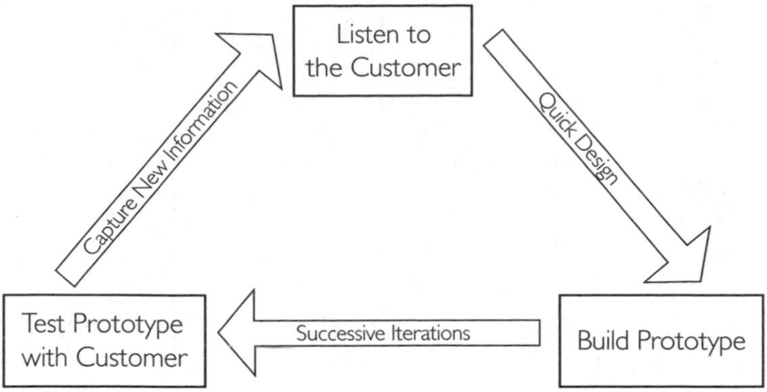

Select the Appropriate Project Life Cycle

The business analyst works collaboratively with the project manager and the technical and business leads to determine the most appropriate project life cycle for use on the project. This essential step ensures the solution development phases, subphases, and deliverables are well-understood prior to planning the requirements elicitation, analysis, and specification activities. When selecting the appropriate project life cycle, we provide two approaches, one based on project strengths and one based on project size, complexity, and risk.

Project Life Cycle Selection Based on Project Strengths

Table 5-1 offers an overall summary of when to use the different project life cycles based on project strengths. The X in a column represents a project's strength. For example, if project strengths include proven processes, project brevity, and stable requirements, choose the waterfall model as project life cycle. The hybrid cycle is, as the name implies, a combination of two or more approaches.[3]

Project Life Cycle Selection Based on Project Size, Complexity, and Risk

The project profile (refer once again to Table 3-1) is also helpful when determining the appropriate project life cycle to use. Consider

Table 5-1—Project Characteristics and Product Cycles

	Waterfall Legacy	RAD	Vee Incremental	Evolutionary Agile	Spiral	Prototype	Hybrid
Proven Processes	X						X
Sufficient Funding						X	
Customer Focus		X	X	X			
Historical Data							
Modern Support Environment		X	X	X	X	X	
Project Brevity	X						
Stable Requirements	X	X					
Strategic Teaming		X					
Team Cohesiveness			X	X			
Team Expertise			X	X	X		
Training Support			X	X	X		X
PM Expertise							X

the following when selecting the project life cycle based on the project profile.[4]

Project Life Cycle for Small, Independent, Low-Risk Projects

The waterfall model is a highly effective project life cycle for short-duration, well-understood projects with stable requirements and few or no dependencies. The waterfall model assumes that events affecting the project are predictable, tools and activities are well-understood, and as a rule, once a phase is complete, it will not be revisited. The waterfall model lays out the steps for development and stresses the importance of requirements. However, keep in mind that projects rarely follow the sequential flow, and customers usually find it difficult to completely state all requirements early in the project.

Project Life Cycle for Medium-Sized, Moderately Complex Projects

As projects become more complicated and more dependencies exist, it is wise to break the work down into manageable components or subprojects delivered incrementally. The challenge is to ensure that the increments can be integrated into a fully functioning solution that meets project objectives. The vee model, which adds the vertical dimension to the waterfall model, altering the waterfall shape into a V shape, is useful for moderately complex projects. At the base of the vee is the component build. Components of the system are developed in increments, and each component produces a partial implementation; functionality is gradually added in subsequent increments.

Project Life Cycle for Large, Highly Complex Projects

Since complex projects are by their very nature less predictable, it is important for the project team to keep its options open, and, indeed, to even build options into the project approach. This keep-our-options-open approach requires a considerable amount of time to be spent on researching and studying the business problem or opportunity; conducting competitive, technological, and benchmark studies; defining dependencies and interrelationships; and identifying all potential options to meet the business need or solve the business problem. In addition, the team analyzes the economic, technical, operational, cultural, and legal feasibility of each solution option until it is clear which option has a highest probability of success.

The model that applies in this situation is the spiral development model, often described as an iterative waterfall approach. In addition, the evolutionary development model can be used, which allows for the implementation of the solution incrementally based on experience and learning from the results of prior versions. Solution functions are prioritized based on business value and, once high-risk areas are resolved, the highest value components are delivered first. This approach may also involve rapid prototyping—a fast build of a solution component to prove an idea is feasible.

Tailor the Project Life Cycle

Once the project life cycle is selected, the core team has all the information needed to tailor the approach to requirements development. *Tailoring* is the process of customizing the project life cycle to meet the unique needs of a particular project. It involves examining the profile of the project once again before selecting the deliverables, activities, and reviews that fit the essential characteristics of the particular project. Tailoring helps evaluate the project life cycle requirements in order to develop optimum plans. Specifically, tailor the project life cycle in order to:

+ Save money

+ Prevent duplication

+ Meet (preserve) the schedule

+ Meet quality expectations

+ Add value

Tailoring applies to both the project and product life cycles. The project manager tailors the project life cycle for the system of planning and control meetings held, the amount of project management documentation produced and maintained, and the general level of rigor and formality. The business analyst tailors the requirements activities within the product life cycle for the number of requirements elicitation events conducted, the number of requirements artifacts produced, the number of control gate reviews conducted to validate requirements, and the general level of rigor and formality.

Determine the Solution Delivery Strategies

There is another factor to consider before finalizing the requirement management plan. In addition to selecting the appropriate project life cycle, there are several delivery strategies to choose from, as listed below.

+ Single development with single delivery

+ Incremental development

  □ Single delivery

  □ Incremental delivery

+ Evolutionary development

  □ Single delivery

  □ Incremental delivery

Table 5-2 provides guidelines for selecting the optimum delivery strategy.

Table 5-2—Solution Delivery Strategies

Use This Approach . . .	When These Characteristics Are Present
Single development with single delivery	• All requirements are known and stable. • Full capability is required with initial deployment. • Funding is available for full development.

Incremental development with a single delivery	• System increments are delivered in phases:
	  ▫ To initiate development of long-lead, critical technology
	  ▫ For cost-effectiveness
	• Increments are developed individually for assembly into a complete system.

Incremental development with incremental deliveries	• Final system requirements and incremental requirements are completely determined beforehand. • Increments are planned, developed, and delivered, allowing for assembly into an operational system that incrementally increases functionality. • Each increment provides early but limited functionality. • Budget limitations and/or incremental funding are accommodated. • Successful integration requires careful requirements definition and design.
Evolutionary development	• All requirements cannot be completely specified beforehand. • Use a trial-and-error process. • The development process itself uncovers unforeseen needs and system applications. • User feedback is essential. • New or enhanced functionality is added to the functioning system at each iteration to satisfy newly discovered needs.

Project Life Cycle Training

Another factor to be taken into account is whether the project team is familiar with the project life cycle that is selected. If the project is using a new development approach, the project manager needs to allocate time and cost for the team members to learn the new development process, tools, and techniques. The first project that implements a new project life cycle will often serve as the pilot. New methods or tools create increased need for training, communication, coaching, and mentoring. The business analyst will also need to plan training time for new users so they can learn how to contribute to elicitation exercises.

Summary

+ Project life cycles are used to help add structure and control points to projects.

+ Project life cycles bring order to and reduce the risk of project activities.

+ Project life cycles provide a repeatable, predictable way to develop products.

+ The project life cycle identifies the technical work that is needed, the roles needed in each phase, and the control gate entry and exit criteria.

+ A complete project life cycle defines the work from project management, business analyst, and IT perspectives.

+ It is essential that the project life cycle is determined and customized in the beginning of a project, prior to the start of requirements activities.

Action Plan for the Business Analyst

+ Enlist the project manager and the business and technical leads to determine the project life cycle and delivery approach to be used for the project.

+ Together, tailor and customize the requirements activities, deliverables, and reviews based on the needs of the project.

Remember that the more unstable and unclear the requirements are, the more rigor and flexibility are needed.

Endnotes

1. Project Management Institute. *A Guide to the Project Management Body of Knowledge*, 3rd ed., 2004. Newtown Square, PA: Project Management Institute, Inc.

2. M. Lippert, S. Roock, H. Wolf, H. Züllighoven. *XP in Complex Project Settings: Some Extensions*, in: Informatik/Informatique. Schweizerischer Verband der Informatikorganisationen. Nr. 2, April, 2002.

3. Richard Bechtold. *Essentials of Software Project Management*, 1999. Vienna, VA: Management Concepts, Inc.

4. Kathleen B. Hass. "Living on the Edge: Managing Project Complexity." Originally published as part of 2007 PMI Global Congress Proceedings North America.

Chapter 6

Plan Requirements Activities

In This Chapter:

- Planning Requirements Activities

- Detailed Requirements Phase Plans

- Summary-Level Requirements Plans For Design, Construction, and Test Activities

- Summary-Level Requirements Plans for Delivery of the New/Changed Business Solution

- Requirements Planning Considerations

- The Requirements Management Plan

Planning Requirements Activities

After the decisions described in Chapter 5 have been made, the business analyst works with the core planning team to capture and record the following information in the requirements management plan:

+ Requirements elicitation activities and deliverables, e.g., interviews, workshops, procedures, surveys, current system reviews. Deliverables include interview notes, workshop output (models, text statements), survey results.

+ Requirements analysis deliverables, e.g., requirements understanding models, diagrams, lists, tables, structured text

+ Requirements specification and documentation deliverables, e.g., user requirements statements, business requirement document, concepts of operations document, initial solution concept document, statement of work, system requirements document, domain, process and data models

+ Requirements management deliverables, e.g., requirements management plan, system engineering management plan, requirements verification and validation plan, requirements traceability and verification plans

+ Requirements verification and validation activities, e.g., requirement artifact quality reviews, user acceptance test activities

It is tempting to plan the requirements elicitation activities only at the beginning of the requirements phase. However, it is risky to focus on only one aspect of requirements development, since plans for later activities may impact the amount of elicitation that is needed. In addition, elicitation activities will likely be conducted in an iterative manner when the business analyst is performing later requirements tasks. Therefore, we recommend a rolling wave approach to planning requirements activities. This means establishing plans for *all activities in the requirements phase at a detailed level* and establishing plans for the requirements activities in the design, construction, test, and deliver phases at a summary level. These plans are then detailed later in the project life cycle. Refer to Figure 6-1 for a depiction of the requirement planning and elicitation activities conducted following the approval of the new project in the Enterprise Analysis phase.

Figure 6-1—Flow of Information into the Requirements Planning and Elicitation Process

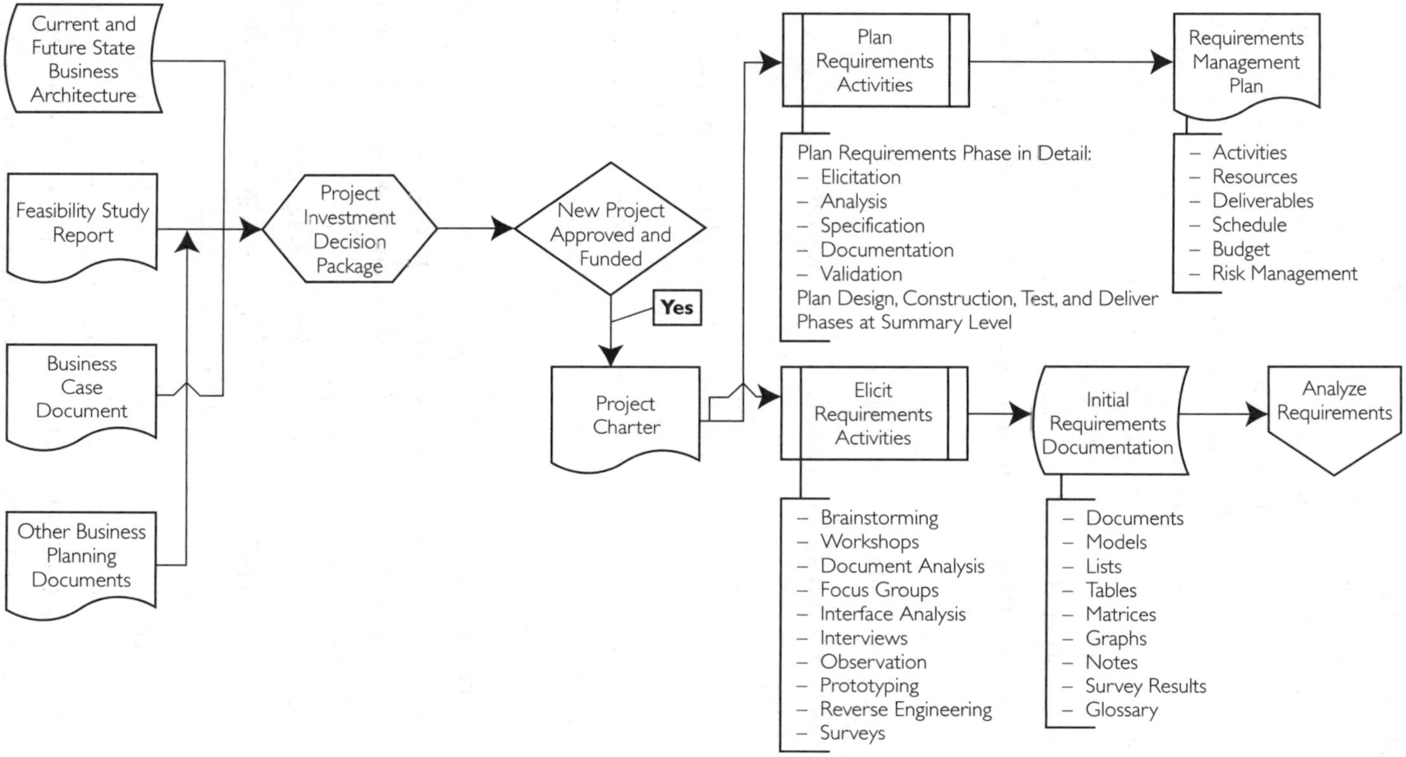

Detailed Requirements Phase Plans

At the beginning of the project, detailed plans are established for all activities in the requirements phase. A synopsis of the resources needed, the activities to be conducted, and the deliverables to be produced is provided for each requirements subphase. See Figure 6-2 for a work breakdown structure (WBS) template depicting the requirement work to be considered when planning requirements activities throughout the project. Based on the project life cycle that has been selected, and the size, complexity, and risk of the project, select the activities that should be performed to ensure project objectives are met.

Requirements Elicitation Planning

When planning for requirements elicitation, consider the following:

+ **Resources.** Identify all stakeholders (end-users, business unit process owners, business unit manager, customers, etc.) that will be involved in the requirements elicitation sessions. In addition, identify the core team that will prepare for and conduct the elicitation activities.

+ **Activities.** Plan for all elicitation sessions with customers, users, and stakeholders to begin the requirements capture process. Typical elicitation activities include stakeholder analysis, requirements workshops, interviews, surveys, workplace observations, focus groups, interface analysis, reverse engineering, prototyping, review of existing system and business documents, and note-taking and feedback loops.

+ **Deliverables.** Identify deliverables that will be produced at the conclusion of each elicitation session. Deliverables may be a stakeholder list accompanied by information about the stakeholders to involve in each elicitation session, interview

Figure 6-2—Requirements Activities WBS

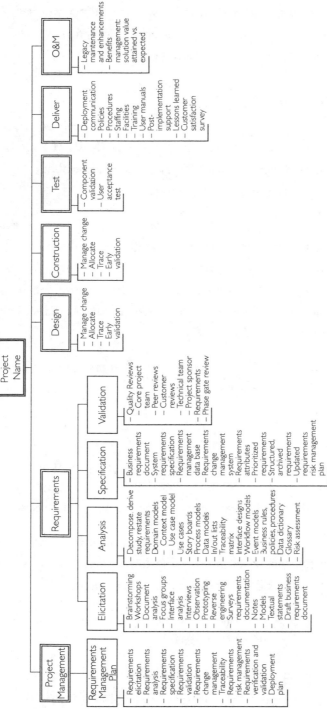

notes, survey response compilation and analysis, workshop results in the form of notes, requirements statements, use cases, scenarios, tables, graphs, and models.

Requirements Analysis Planning

Establish plans for all requirements analysis activities. Refer to *Getting It Right: Business Requirement Analysis Tools and Techniques*, another volume in this series, for detailed information about requirements analysis activities and deliverables.

- **Resources.** Bring together a small core team of business and technology experts who will be involved in analyzing and progressively elaborating the business requirements. This team will likely be composed of some of the same members who conducted elicitation; however, expert modelers and tool users may need to be added.

- **Activities.** Plan for all activities that will take place to analyze the information captured during elicitation sessions, including some or all of the following:

  - Structure requirements information into various categories, evaluate requirements for selected qualities, represent requirements in different forms, derive detailed requirements from high-level requirements, and negotiate priorities.

  - Determine required function and performance characteristics, the context of implementation, stakeholder constraints and measures of effectiveness, and validation criteria.

  - Decompose and capture requirements in a combination of text and graphical formats.

  - Study requirements feasibility to determine if each requirement is viable legally, culturally, technically, operationally, and economically; trade off requirements to determine the most feasible requirement alternatives.

▫ Assess requirements risks and constraints and modify requirements to mitigate identified risks.

▫ Model requirements to restate and clarify them. (Note that text statements are appropriate when precise definitions are needed and that graphical representations are preferred when sequence and timing are required. Sometimes simple tables or lists suffice.)

▫ Derive additional requirements as more is learned about the business need.

▫ Prioritize requirements to reflect the fact that not all requirements are of equal value to the business.

▫ As requirements are decomposed and restated, conduct feedback sessions with those who provided the requirements.

✦ **Deliverables.** Identify all deliverables that will be produced at the conclusion of each analysis activity. Identify the number and types of models, documents, tables, lists, matrices.

Requirements Specification and Documentation Planning

Establish plans for all requirements specification activities. Refer to *Getting It Right: Business Requirement Analysis Tools and Techniques* for detailed information about requirements specification and documentation activities and deliverables.

✦ **Resources.** Bring together a small core team of business and technology experts who will be involved in specification of the business requirements. This is likely to be a subset of the original core requirements team.

- **Activities.** Plan for all specification activities:

  □ Elaborate and structure requirement specifications, providing a repository of requirements with a complete attribute set.

  □ Through the process of specification and progressive elaboration, the requirements team often detects areas that are not defined in sufficient detail, which if not addressed can lead to uncontrolled change to system requirements.

  □ Identify all the precise attributes of each requirement. Doing so ensures an understanding of the source, criticality, risk, priority, and relative importance of each unique requirement.

- **Deliverables.** Identify deliverables that will be produced at the conclusion of each specification activity. The system specification document(s) or database that archives all requirement information is the key output of the requirements specification process.

Requirements Validation and Requirements Phase Exit Planning

Establish plans for all requirements validation and phase exit activities. Refer to *Getting It Right: Business Requirement Analysis Tools and Techniques* for detailed information about requirements validation and phase exit activities and deliverables.

- **Resources.** Bring together small focus groups of business and technology experts to validate the business requirements.

- **Activities.** Plan for all validation and phase exit activities, including:

  □ Quality review sessions with focus groups of business and technology experts.

- □ A formal control gate review to gain approval to baseline the requirement set and formally control subsequent requirements changes, exit the requirements phase, and proceed to solution design and construction.

- ◆ **Deliverables.** Identify deliverables that will be produced at the conclusion of the requirements phase:

  - □ Updated project schedule, cost, and scope estimates (made by the project manager), and business case (made by the business analyst), to provide the information needed for management to determine whether continued investment in the project is warranted

  - □ Baselined requirements; a method to trace requirements through development, verification, and validation plans; and a formal requirements change control process to manage changes to requirements

Summary-Level Requirements Plans for Design, Construction, and Test Activities

Establish high-level plans for all requirements activities performed during design, construction, and test phases.

- ◆ **Resources.** Establish a small business analysis team that works with the design and development team to manage requirements throughout the development life cycle.

- ◆ **Activities.** Plan for all requirements management activities:

  - □ Allocating requirements to different subsystems or subcomponents of the system.

  - □ Tracing requirements throughout system design and development to track where in the system each requirement is satisfied.

□ Managing changes and enhancements to the requirements to add, delete, and modify requirements during all project phases.

□ Continually validating and verifying requirements with requirements sources throughout the project.

♦ **Deliverables.** Identify deliverables that will be produced during the design, construction, and test phases. These deliverables might include documented change requests, implemented changes to requirements, and requirements traceability confirmation.

Summary-Level Requirements Plans for Delivery of the Business Solution

Establish plans to prepare the business and technical communities to accept and operate the new business solution and to measure the business benefits achieved.

♦ **Resources.** Establish a small team of business and technical experts that will build plans to establish readiness to accept and operate the new business solution.

♦ **Activities.** Plan for all requirements solution deployment activities:

□ Business operations: transitioning from the old to the new business policies, processes, tools, application systems and technologies; designing and developing training, organizational structuring, staffing, facilities, desktop tools, communications, etc.

□ Technical operations: transitioning from development to operations environments; designing and developing training, organizational structuring, staffing, facilities, infrastructure hardware and software, communications, etc.

▫ Metrics and measurement system to determine the business benefits of the new solution.

♦ **Deliverables.** Identify deliverables that will be produced to manage the deployment of the new business system, including memos, e-mails, training sessions, training manuals, user manuals, operations manuals, etc. In addition, plan for the development of the measurement system to determine the benefits attained by the organization from the new business solution, including measurement collection, analysis, and reporting system.

Requirements Planning Considerations

Several barriers may arise when planning requirements activities. These barriers include:

♦ **Distributed, culturally diverse users.** Users and team members are not co-located and do not speak the same business language.

♦ **Difficulty getting user involvement.** Understand and keep in mind that users, sponsors, and customers must continue to support business operations while attending requirements elicitation sessions.

♦ **Difficulty articulating requirements.** It requires a very different skill set to describe a business process than to operate it.

The business analyst works collaboratively with all key business and technical stakeholders to overcome these barriers to success.

The Requirements Management Plan

The *requirements management plan* (RMP) is an agreement between the project manager, the business analyst, the project sponsor, and all key project stakeholders on not only the requirements elicitation approach, but also on the methods for requirements analysis, specification, documentation, and validation. All decisions made by the core team during the requirements planning process are documented in the RMP. This plan helps to ensure that the funds are secured and the time is scheduled to complete requirements-related tasks and identifies the subject matter experts that will need to be made available for elicitation and validation activities. The RMP serves as a key communication tool for the business analyst and project manager. It is first used to secure the business and technical resources needed to complete the early requirements activities. The resources in the business units or the field may not be readily available to participate in interviews and workshops unless plans are developed and approved by management. Sufficient time needs to be provided for organizations to free the resources that are best suited to provide the needed expertise. An example of the potential complexity when global teams are involved for one task is illustrated in Table 6-1.

Benefits of the Requirements Management Plan

The RMP becomes the roadmap for requirements documentation and management throughout the life of the project. There are other names for this plan, such as *business analyst work division strategy* or *business analyst work plan*. Key benefits of an RMP are:

+ Communicating the requirements activities that will be completed and who will be responsible or involved in the process

+ Ensuring that users, sponsors, customers, and developers have a common understanding of the requirements-related work

+ Serving as an agreement on tasks that require funding and scheduling in the project management plan

Table 6-1—Sample Requirements Elicitation Task Information

Task	Business Analyst	Business User	Standards and Template Location
Process analysis of the cash-to-quote process	Jose	USA: Sally (Primary) 3 wks duration/30 hours with an additional 4 hours to review completed documentation Asia-Pacific: Thomas 2 wks duration/15 hours with an additional 2 hours to review completed documentation EMEA: Henry 2 wks duration/15 hours with an additional 2 hours to review completed documentation Latin America: Maria 2 wks duration/15 hours with an additional 2 hours to review completed documentation	1) As-is process description 2) As-is text description tied to Q1 pain point customer survey 3) Identification of high-level use cases with actors, alternative flows, exceptions

+ Drawing the line on what requirements can be included in the time allocated

+ Narrowing the expectation gap at the beginning of the project rather than later, when it is too late to make adjustments

> Seven Ps: Prior proper planning prevents pretty poor performance.
>
> *Cleve B. Pillifant, Executive Director*
> *Project Management Division*
> *Management Concepts*

Relationship to Project Management Plan

Unfortunately, most teams don't use an RMP. Without it, business analysts are neglecting to use a valuable tool that contributes significantly toward delivering the project on time, on budget, and within the expected scope.

> The RMP is neither the project management plan nor the requirements themselves.

The requirements management plan is a subsidiary to the project management plan (PMP), but is typically a separate document. The variances between the two plans are shown in Table 6-2.

After the RMP has been reviewed and approved by the project sponsor, changes are to be made in a controlled manner. The RMP

Table 6-2—Variances between the PMP and the RMP

Project Management Plan	Requirements Management Plan
Primary project control document for baselining budget, time and scope assumptions, and constraints	Subsidiary element of the project management plan
Owned by the project manager	Owned by the business analyst
Documents project management objectives to meet schedule, cost, time, and scope	Documents product objectives throughout the project life cycle

not only defines requirements elicitation, analysis, and documentation activities, but also supports requirements verification and validation and requirements change management.

Requirements Management Plan Elements

As a formal project document, the RMP provides several key pieces of information:

+ The methods, tools, and techniques to be used

+ The identified stakeholders and users to be involved

+ The elicitation, analysis, specification, documentation, and validation activities

+ The requirements artifacts to be created, e.g., documents, models, tables, lists

+ The process to manage changes to requirements during design, construction, test, and delivery

A typical RMP table of contents is shown in Figure 6-3. See Appendix C for a sample RMP template.

Requirements Management Plan Approval

Successful business analysts gain an agreement in advance on the scope of business analysis activities. As you can see by the sample RMP depicted in Figure 6-3, there are a significant amount of requirements activities that can be conducted. The business analyst is cautioned to plan requirements activities that will be completed to gain an understanding of the requirements that is *just good enough* to proceed to design.

> Requirements are owned by the customer.

Figure 6-3—A Typical Table of Contents for an RMP

Requirements Management Plan

Introduction
1. Project Name and Brief Scope Description
2. Overview of Requirements Standards
3. Related Documents

Stakeholders
4. Stakeholder Listing

Users
5. User Listing

Requirements Deliverables and Required Attributes
6. Deliverables by phase
7. Required attributes for each deliverable

Verification and Validation Process
8. Allocation Process (if applicable)
9. Traceability Process
10. Peer Review Process
11. Customer Review Process
12. Management Review Process

Change Management Process
13. Requirements Change Management Overview

Requirements Risk Assessment Process
14. Requirements Risk Management Overview

Resource Estimates
15. Requirements estimates by deliverable

Environmental Needs and Responsibilities
16. Requirements-related Project Environmental Needs and Responsibilities
17. Appendixes
    i. Sign-off
    ii. Revision Control

The project manager and business analyst secure the approval of the project sponsor, formally agreeing to the planned requirements activities. It is best to have a formal meeting between the project team and the sponsor, customers, and users to present how requirements will be gathered. The goal of this session is to secure allocation of time for business and technical representatives to participate in the elicitation process.

Summary

+ The RMP is a formal project plan that describes the requirements process used on the project.

+ The RMP is a communication tool to propose requirements activities. Once approved, it becomes the work plan for requirements tasks.

+ The RMP is used to secure agreement between the project team and the key stakeholders on their participation in the requirements process.

+ Key elements in the RMP are:

  □ Description of project scope, applicable standards, and related documents

  □ Stakeholder and user identification

  □ Requirements deliverables and mandatory attributes

  □ Verification and validation process

  □ Requirements change management process

  □ Requirements-related risks

  □ Resource estimates for completing requirements tasks

  □ Capital and expense requests

Action Plan for the Business Analyst

+ Identify examples of the issues associated with the requirements planning processes that have been encountered in the past.

+ Detect if the process problems are associated with lack of planning for the requirements activities.

+ Prepare a requirements management plan for the next project.

Part III
Elicitation in Practice

*H*istorically, organizations have not understood the value of investing significant amounts of time and cost to involve the customer, end-user, and business process owner throughout the project life cycle. Indeed, the pressure to deliver projects faster has never been greater. However, we are beginning to understand the consequences of abbreviated requirements activities. Hooks and Farry[1] state that more than 80 percent of all product defects are introduced in the requirements phase. Professional business analysts employ targeted elicitation practices to improve requirements quality and eliminate requirements defects early in the project life cycle.

The business analyst needs to select elicitation activities that provide the best opportunity for information exchange. There are several considerations that influence the choice of elicitation techniques, including project cost and time constraints, the availability of participants, the culture of the organization, and the requirements deliverables to be produced. The goal is to *right size* the amount of rigor used for requirements elicitation for each project. Although mature organizations provide tools and templates to guide requirements elicitation sessions, the project team needs to consider tailoring the approach to the unique needs of the project. Scheduling too many elicitation sessions is a process and resource waste. Too few sessions may result in missing, incomplete, or inaccurate requirements that are identified later in the project life cycle. In this case, the project schedule and budget are at risk because planning for the adequate number of sessions was not considered earlier.

To be successful in this endeavor, the business analyst needs to become knowledgeable and skilled in all elicitation techniques, understanding their strengths and weaknesses, and plan for just the right amount of rigor.

> Talking to project stakeholders is mandatory. Talking to them with a purposeful elicitation plan is a learned skill.

The elicitation process can be referred to as *requirements gathering, requirements definition,* or *requirements discovery.* The best practice is to define the terms used in the environment and consistently use the same term with all stakeholders in formal and informal communication. This part of the book discusses elicitation, but there are some key considerations to mention first:

+ When conducting elicitation sessions, the business analyst starts the meeting by reviewing the importance of the project; its strategic alignment; the objectives, scope, assumptions, and constraints; and expected business benefits so that all participants understand the significance and urgency of the endeavor. Inputs to the elicitation process that provide this information may include:

   □ Business case

   □ Project charter

   □ Feasibility study

   □ Stakeholder analysis

   □ User analysis

   □ Approved requirements management plan (RMP)

- Elicitation activities are performed concurrently with the initiation and planning processes described in *The PMBOK® Guide*.

- The output of elicitation is the first iteration of the business requirements document (BRD) accompanied by supporting information that is further elaborated and decomposed during requirements analysis and specification.

- Design, construction, and test activities have not begun, although a high-level solution concept was developed during Enterprise Analysis activities.

- Elicitation does not occur only in the requirements phase, but continues throughout the business solution life cycle as additional requirements are derived or discovered and formally added through the change management process.

The elicitation process is dependent on access to the user groups. Some dispersed global groups may be accessible only through a survey. Other groups will be involved minimally if they have been deemed of low importance or are peripheral to the business area undergoing change. Others may be involved in multiple elicitation sessions and feedback loops. Refer to the figure on the next page, which demonstrates the iterative interaction between the business analyst and user groups.

Many elicitation techniques are available for use by the business analyst; however, only a few are generally recognized as the most effective and appropriate for general use. In this part, we discuss the most commonly used techniques. For each technique we present common variations, key rules for effective use of the technique, and guidelines for tailoring the technique to the project characteristics.

- In Chapter 7 we present the most commonly used requirements elicitation technique, brainstorming.

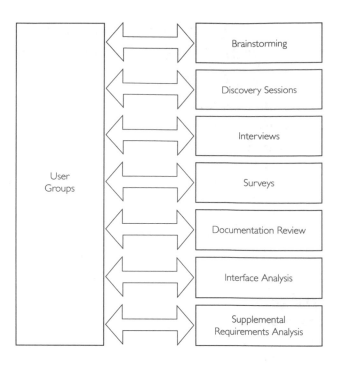

- In Chapter 8 we discuss how the business analyst plans and facilitates the most rigorous requirements elicitation techniques, facilitated workshops and discovery sessions.

- In Chapter 9 we present interviewing techniques.

- In Chapter 10 we discuss the value and usefulness of surveys.

- In Chapter 11 we discuss documentation reviews.

- In Chapter 12 we discuss the importance of analyzing interfaces.

- In Chapter 13 we discuss the techniques for identifying supplemental requirements.

Refer to *The Art and Power of Facilitation: Running Powerful Meetings*, another volume in the Business Analysis Essential Library series, for a detailed presentation of tools and techniques that can be used to successfully prepare for and facilitate requirements elicitation sessions.

Endnotes

1. Ivy F. Hooks and Kristin A. Farry. *Customer Centered Products: Creating Successful Products Through Smart Requirements Management*, 2000. New York: American Management Association.

Chapter 7

Brainstorming

In This Chapter:

- Types of Brainstorming
- Rules for Brainstorming
- Tailoring Brainstorming Sessions

Brainstorming is a group facilitation technique that is used often in elicitation sessions to generate ideas, approaches, and issues. Brainstorming is a creative process that allows participants to look for solutions that may not have been previously considered. Brainstorming harnesses the power of the group and is used for both idea generation and problem solving. The process brings together a group of subject matter experts who possess the requisite domain knowledge to solve complex problems and focus on innovative solutions. This process is invaluable to the business analyst, since business problems are increasingly complex and interrelated, thus requiring the contribution of multiple experts with diverse skills and perspectives to understand.

Brainstorming is also used as a consensus-building technique. Using brainstorming for consensus building is effective when the decision is such that all groups need to support the decision after leaving the session. Brainstorming advantages and disadvantages—from the business analyst perspective—are shown in Table 7-1.

Table 7-1—Brainstorming Advantages and Disadvantages

Advantages of Brainstorming	Disadvantages of Brainstorming
• Generates multiple ideas quickly • Involves multiple perspectives • Promotes equal participation	• Ideas are not discussed or explored • The true meaning may be ambiguous or misunderstood

Types of Brainstorming

Types of brainstorming include:

+ **Individual.** A project team member creates a list of ideas concerning a project issue or risk.

+ **Open.** Meeting participants call out ideas that are captured by the meeting facilitator or scribe. This is an efficient process when team dynamics are good and individual skill sets are strong.

+ **Structured.** Meeting participants silently write down their ideas and the facilitator then requests that each person in turn share just one idea. The meeting continues with all the participants taking their turn until new ideas are exhausted. This is an effective process when a strong personality or a person with higher position or expert power is in the group. All participants can contribute equally, as this method allows introverts time to silently think through their position before being distracted by other meeting participants.

Rules for Brainstorming

Key rules for brainstorming meetings are:

+ Make a decision on the type of brainstorming, open or structured. This decision is usually made by the facilitator, typically the business analyst.

+ Clearly state the objective of the meeting. For example, state (and write on a flip chart or white board) that the meeting objective is to "Create options for increasing Asia/Pacific user involvement in our elicitation and analysis activities."

+ Create an environment in which participants feel encouraged to participate and believe that their time is used effectively.

+ Establish ground rules at the beginning of the session:

  □ Do not discuss ideas during the brainstorming session.

  □ Do not dismiss an idea.

  □ Do not discount a person or an idea.

  □ The only discussion allowed is questions to clarify the idea.

  □ Do build on others' suggestions and ideas.

  □ Do have fun.

  □ Do give rewards for the craziest idea.

+ Establish roles:

  □ A timekeeper

  □ A scribe who captures the ideas

  □ A facilitator who runs the meeting. If the project size is large and the requirements risk is high, the business analyst might decide to enlist the help of a professional facilitator to conduct the meeting.

+ Determine the process to be used for combining like ideas and categorizing and summarizing the brainstorm results, e.g., multivoting.

+ Publish an agenda.

+ Create multiple meetings if the issue is complex and requires a break to reduce meeting fatigue.

+ Schedule follow-up meetings.

+ Use internal resources (such as senior business analysts and senior business process improvement experts) to help sort the categories on large projects.

+ Use prioritization techniques to sort ideas. Votes can be given to team members to indicate their choice for the top ideas to consider taking forward for more analysis.

Tailoring Brainstorm Sessions

The business analyst considers the environmental factors, such as organizational culture and project criticality, when deciding how many sessions are needed or to ensure all good ideas have been identified. The business analyst scales brainstorming activities to the project environment. Table 7-2 shows the brainstorming variances scaled to the project profile.

Table 7-2—Brainstorming Scaled to Project Size, Risk, Complexity

Elicitation Technique	Project Profile		
	Small Independent Low Risk	Medium Moderately Complex Some Risk	Large Highly Complex Significant Risk
Brainstorming	Use informally during project meetings.	Schedule separate meetings with impacted stakeholders.	Secure trained resources to set up and run the facilitated sessions and follow-on actions.

Chapter 8

Requirements Elicitation Workshops and Discovery Sessions

In This Chapter:

- Resolving Requirement Conflicts

- Formal Requirements Elicitation Workshops

- Business Process Improvement Workshops

- Agile Requirements Elicitation Workshops

- Rapid Application Design Workshops

- Joint Application Development Workshops

- Rules for Elicitation Workshops

- Tips for Successful Workshops

- Tailoring Requirements Elicitation Workshops

Structured facilitated requirements workshops, which are formal sessions involving multiple groups, such as end-users, subject matter experts, the project manager, and business and IT representatives, are common. Their goal is to elicit requirements from the group of multiskilled and diverse participants. The output of the session may be text, graphical, or matrix documentation. Workshops can be used to elicit, specify, refine, quality-check, and reach closure on business requirements.

Resolving Requirement Conflicts

The requirements workshop is most effective when the multiple business areas are undergoing change and are cross-functional in nature. In this case, it is important to understand and resolve conflicts and inconsistencies among diverse perspectives. Meeting with key stakeholders in the same room and hearing different perspectives ensures requirements are complete, and therefore improves requirements quality. Resolving requirements conflicts early in the project is essential to reducing requirements defects that have the potential to adversely impact the success of the project during solution delivery. See Figure 8-1, which depicts the relationship between project conflict and progress.

Requirements workshops facilitate understanding what the project is really trying to accomplish from a business perspective, because the key business stakeholders are in the room contributing. When conflict emerges, remember that conflict can often be positive when handled well, as the participants mutually determine the tradeoffs that must be made. The workshop process contributes to resolving disconnects and clarifying the scope of requirements that can

Figure 8-1—Relationship between Project Conflict and Progress

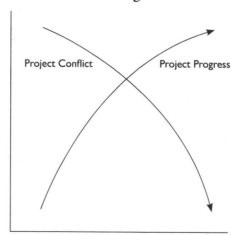

Project Conflict   Project Progress

realistically be accomplished within the time and cost constraints in early stages of the project. In addition, workshop sessions facilitate discussion on whether the project objectives are technically feasible, since both business and IT subject matter experts are present. From the perspective of a business analyst, the strengths and weaknesses of facilitated workshop sessions are those shown in Table 8-1.

Requirements workshops and collaborative discovery sessions are generally any type of meeting through which end-users are highly involved in creating or influencing the direction of the solution design and development. Many product development methodologies and improvement approaches use team-based approaches, from informal discovery sessions, to joint design sessions, to formal workshops involving key project participants to understand requirements. Facilitated elicitation workshops are designed to increase the collaboration between the business and technical teams, and are described below.

Table 8-1—Benefits versus Disadvantages of Elicitation Workshop Sessions

Benefits of Elicitation Workshops	Disadvantages of Elicitation Workshops
• Effective at getting at real requirements rather than perceived requirements • Can neutralize a predominate voice by creating ground rules for discussion and decision-making • A greater chance of obtaining consensus is created because stakeholders are presented with the issues and questions at the same time • Feedback is immediate—the facilitator's interpretation is documented for immediate stakeholder confirmation • Successfully gather requirements from a large group in a short period of time • Documentation is completed within hours of the session and provided quickly to participants for their review	• Difficulty in getting appropriate stakeholders in one room at same time • Increased number of global projects poses logistic difficulties and adds complexity • Success of the session is highly dependent on the expertise of the facilitator • Can be expensive

Formal Requirements Elicitation Workshops

Formal requirements elicitation workshops are structured meetings in which a carefully selected group of stakeholders and content experts works together to define, create, refine, and reach closure on deliverables (such as models and documents) that represent business requirements for a new/changed business system. Successful workshops encourage teamwork, communication, decision-making, and mutual understanding of the business requirements.

Workshops are also an effective way to bring together customers, users, and solution suppliers to improve the quality of the product without sacrificing time to delivery. These sessions tend to commit users to the requirements definition process and promote their sense of ownership of the deliverables and, ultimately, of the new solution.[1] Workshops typically start at a broad level, identifying the scope of the requirements, then move on to establishing high-level business functions or processes, and then go into detailed business scenarios.

For projects using iterative development techniques, initial workshops focus on high-risk and high-value requirements, and immediately get started on development of the first increment of the solution. In addition, smaller, informal discovery sessions are used. This approach reduces the risk of trying to identify all the requirement at the beginning of the project. It must be noted, however, that enough high-level requirements definition must be completed to be able to establish the initial release plan.

Business Process Improvement Workshops

A business process improvement session is a type of formal requirements elicitation workshop during which an analysis of existing business processes is conducted with the goal of implementing process improvements. The business process is analyzed using techniques described in Six Sigma, which is a highly structured program for improving business processes, or any method that systemically looks at process inputs, process steps, and outputs to model the current state.

Typically a "cards on the wall" approach is used, mapping the current business process for all to see. The group then looks for opportunities to improve the process by better aligning it with the current environment and customer needs. The process is then changed, and the performance of the process is measured and continually tuned to bring performance within identified tolerances. Business process improvement is also referred to as *business process reengineering, process quality management,* and *continuous process improvement.*

Agile Requirements Elicitation Workshops

Agile methods minimize the risk of requirements defects caused by inadequate stakeholder participation by working daily with the customer and delivering small increments of functionality, and gaining requirements feedback after each increment. Agile development teams do not typically conduct large, formal requirements workshops; agile teams prefer to operate in smaller working group sessions. However, a formal workshop may be needed to document the scope of the requirements and to determine the number and sequence of the increments.

The tools used for initial modeling sessions can vary by proponent and vendor, but generally the tools are aligned to the Unified Modeling Language (UML™), a language for specifying, constructing, visualizing, and documenting the artifacts of a software-intensive system, creating use cases that either graphically or in a text format document the interaction between the user and the new or modified system. The business analyst's role in agile requirements discovery sessions can vary from facilitating the group to getting out of their way; however, the business analyst is always re-examining the business case to make sure the project investment remains sound.

eXtreme Programming (XP) Agile Methodology

eXtreme Programming (XP) is a code-centric agile methodology of project activity and the most prominent of the agile methods.

Requirement elicitation sessions involve users writing stories that capture the features needed by the business community on index cards. This approach acknowledges that ongoing changes to requirements are inevitable, natural, and even desirable, and being able to adapt to changing requirements is better than attempting to define all requirements at the beginning of the project.

Scrum Agile Methodology

Scrum is an agile method that focuses on a collaborative team effort between product champions and IT development teams. The schedule is driven by a prioritized feature list that directs development activities in an iterative fashion. Iterations are referred to as *sprints*, indicating the speed with which iterations of the solution are built. A feature is defined as a user-facing component of the solution that adds value to the business; therefore, the feature list is prioritized based on business value.

Rapid Application Design Workshops

Rapid application design (RAD) standards are drawn from the principles of incremental development emphasizing constant feedback from customers to facilitate capturing requirements and quickly turning them into working components of the solution. The focus is on delivering value and keeping communication open. The goal is to minimize the time between concept and implementation. RAD relies extensively on user involvement, joint application design workshops, prototyping, and the use of CASE (computer-aided systems engineering and application development) tools. RAD often uses highly structured working sessions that may involve team-based analysis, design, and development.

Joint Application Development Workshops

Joint application development (JAD) is a solution development process that brings together developers and end-users to cooperatively develop requirements. The goal is to reduce project delays associated with talking with each user individually and then attempting to pull together a vision of how to develop a satisfactory solution.

> All project life cycles capture requirements.

Rules for Elicitation Workshops

Key rules for formal elicitation workshops and more informal discovery sessions are:

+ Make a decision on the type of session that is appropriate for the project life cycle selected, the organizational culture and standards, project characteristics, and team composition. However, if the project is large, complex, and high risk, consider enlisting the help of a professional facilitator who is trained and well-versed in conducting requirements elicitation workshops and capturing the workshop results.

+ Be clear on what the session will deliver. Ensure that IT requirements are considered when planning the elicitation session to reduce errors in translation during analysis and design activities. Common topics for workshop discussions include:

  □ **Events.** In software product development, an event is defined as something that causes a change in the environment that the proposed business solution must respond too. Examples include:

  – Time: Jobs need to be kicked off at midnight; payroll executes every other Friday

  – Requests: People request cash from an ATM; user presses "Submit" on an enterprise portal; a satellite receives a transmission from mission control

- **Actors.** An actor is a system or person that interacts with the proposed business solution. Examples include:

  - People: Soldiers interacting with equipment; the public requesting information from an agency enterprise portal; senior executives requesting financial analytical reports

  - Systems: An interface to dependent systems such as payroll pulling active employees from the human resource system or an online payment acceptance system requesting and receiving a credit card authorization

- A **process for gathering requirements.** Either a business process flow or a structured development process (covered in the previous section).

Tips for Successful Workshops

Create a plan to address known project challenges that have prevented project success in the past. Discovery sessions are not typically used for general training to address gaps in skill set. However, if the team needs training on subjects as diverse as conflict management or on a specific modeling technique that will be used in the session, find a way to address this need. Develop a training module that is part of the agenda or is a prerequisite to attendance at the session. Prerequisite training is not intended to create a barrier to participation, but to address the challenges unique to the requirements elicitation process. Create a plan for each of these skill-gap barriers to effective team interaction:

- Technical tools, e.g., use cases, CRC cards, CASE tools

- Team or skill development issues, e.g., facilitation skills, brainstorming, communication skills, cross-cultural communication awareness, consensus decision-making

- Requirements elicitation training. Business analysts do not simply write down what customers articulate. Requirements meetings need to probe, often using powerful modeling tools that capture all the users and events that interact in the business process undergoing change. Business analysts must uncover what is *not* said and what is only *implied*, i.e. requirements that are derived as a result of what was said.

- The session is led by a trained facilitator, assisted by a scribe whose role is to document the workshop results. Participants include:

  - *Users:* Individuals who are authorized to speak for their business or mission domain and who can make binding decisions for the project

  - *Developers:* Key individuals responsible for design, construction, or test of the solution and who can provide high-level architecture answers that speak to the technical feasibility of implementing requirements

  - *Subject matter experts:* Process or technology experts who are able to provide immediate process, economic, or technical feasibility assessments to resolve meeting conflicts or roadblocks

  - *Senior managers:* Individuals with the authority to commit organizational funds and make real-time binding vision and direction decisions or tradeoffs

- Limit the meeting to key project participants. If project participants cannot be limited, either the project scope or the meeting agenda is not right sized.

Tailoring Requirements Elicitation Workshops

Discovery sessions are necessary and valuable for virtually any initiative size. However, they can be quite expensive. The business analyst scales the session activities to the project needs. Table 8-2 shows workshop variances scaled to the project profile.

Table 8-2—Workshop Sessions Scaled to Project Size, Risk, Complexity

Elicitation Technique	Project Profile		
	Small Independent Low Risk	Medium Moderately Complex Some Risk	Large Highly Complex Significant Risk
Formal and Information Workshops & Discovery Sessions	Best handled with informal working sessions	Formal meetings with predefined deliverables	Formal meetings with budgets and timelines for securing stakeholder approval on predefined deliverables

Endnote

1. Ellen Gottesdiener. *Requirements by Collaboration*, 2002. Boston: Addison Wesley.

Chapter 9

Interviewing

In This Chapter:

- Requirements Elicitation Interview Types

- Benefits of Requirements Elicitation Interviews

- Tips for Successful Requirements Elicitation Interviews

- Rules for Effective Requirements Elicitation Interviews

- Tailoring Requirements Elicitation Interviews

Interviewing is a systematic, objective method for quickly collecting information from a person or group of people in an informal or formal setting by asking scripted questions. The primary purpose is to gain an understanding of high-level needs, constraints, and assumptions. Interviews are designed to address some of the communication challenges that either cause delay in getting requirements from stakeholders or cause a decrease in the quality of the information gathered. These communication challenges include:

- Inadequate information provided to the project team

- Too much information in a form that cannot be understood by a key stakeholder

+ Unaddressed cultural differences

+ Perceptions and personalities of presenters and stakeholders

+ Technical vocabulary usage

+ Filtering of information based on the experience of the facilitator

+ Preoccupation of the stakeholder due to other messages conflicting with the presentation

+ Lack of openness and trust between project stakeholders

Requirements Elicitation Interview Types

Several different types of interview approaches are commonly used on projects, including:

+ *Personal interviews* are sessions in which scripted questions are asked, with the answers documented. This approach uses exploratory questions on topics that might change requirements, create new requirements, or uncover assumptions, constraints, and/or business rules. Interviews are not typically used to document voluminous information that is considered background and context setting.

+ *Job shadowing* involves walking through a workday with a target user group or watching an individual user perform a specific job task.

+ *Customer site visits* can be useful in understanding the operational environment in which the end-user performs. The goal is to discover prerequisites for job success, preconditions for tasks, or specific business rules that govern job execution.

+ *Task analysis* involves asking end-users to walk through their current jobs. Users can provide work instructions that are useful in describing the current or as-is process. As in interviews, the observer uses exploratory questions to understand what works well and what doesn't work well in the current environment. The goal is to identify the essential tasks or the most frequent tasks. Ways to enable these tasks become priority features for any new or enhanced solution.

Benefits of Requirements Elicitation Interviews

Skilled interviewers adapt the interview to the current situation and improve the quality of the project information by understanding that interviews provide a context to see and decode both verbal and nonverbal information provided by stakeholders. *Verbal* communication is what literally is said or communicated in words during the interview. *Nonverbal* communication is how the information is relayed, including the tone and pacing of words, body language and facial expressiveness, eye movement, and the body gestures or postures that accompany the actual words expressed during the interview.

Interviews can be used to uncover conflicts and discrepancies about stated needs or requirements. This is accomplished by using a problem-probing manner, not a confrontational style. In addition, interviewing can be used to secure agreement from stakeholders that existing requirements documentation is accurate. Table 9-1 shows the benefits versus the disadvantages of elicitation interviews.

Tips for Successful Requirements Elicitation Interviews

Business analysts can improve their ability to read and interpret both verbal and nonverbal communication and build rapport with stakeholders by following the recommendations that follow. To improve verbal communication:

+ Ask prepared questions to gather information consistently.

Table 9-1—Benefits versus Disadvantages of Elicitation Interviews

Benefits of Elicitation Interviews	Disadvantages of Elicitation Interviews
• Allow for interviewer and participant to have scripted discussion points for consistent interpretation of results • Promote interactive discussions to explore detailed information • Encourage participation and build relationships by establishing rapport with stakeholder • Enable observations of nonverbal behavior • Allow immediate follow-up to ensure understanding	• Require access and commitment of stakeholders • Require training and preparation to conduct effective interviews • Require special skills if using unstructured interview techniques • Transcription and analysis of interview data can be complex and expensive • Resulting documentation is subject to interpretation of the interviewer • Stakeholders have difficulty describing the future needs, so the focus is often limited to the current situation

+ Match the pace of the interviewees. If they are cautious, talk slowly. If they are in a hurry, talk quickly.

+ Check understanding often.

+ Ask for examples of their issues and document screen shots or names of stakeholders with particular challenges.

+ Let interviewees know what will be done with the information.

To improve nonverbal listening behavior:

+ Display interest in the subject.

+ Listen for the person's perspective.

+ Respect the person's time by not being late to the interview or running over.

Know how to listen, and you will profit even from those who talk badly.

Plutarch, Greek biographer and moralist (46 AD–120 AD)

Rules for Effective Requirements Elicitation Interviews

The business analyst should keep several rules in mind when conducting interviews:

- ✦ Make a decision on the type and number of interviews. This decision is usually governed by the business objectives, access to senior stakeholders, and schedule and budget constraints. Plan the interviews to secure just enough information to move on.

- ✦ Schedule interviews in advance, as getting on someone's calendars can take days or even weeks.

- ✦ Prepare for the interview by creating open-ended questions. This is one of the most difficult parts of the interview process. Avoid forming questions that may present judgment or a conclusion. See Table 9-2 for sample closed and open-ended questions.

- ✦ Prepare and document the format for the interview. The documentation typically contains the following information:

  ▫ Name of interviewee

Table 9-2—Closed Versus Open-Ended Questions

Closed Question	Reworded Open-Ended Question
"Do you like the current system?" Issue: This might elicit a yes or no answer, and then you need to quickly create another question.	"Tell me about how you use the system (or product or service)?" This encourages them to talk in their language about what they do.
"Tell me the steps you use to create a purchase order." Issue: There is no question here. The interviewee may feel defensive, as if he has to prove he does know the steps.	"Can you describe the process used to create a purchase order?" This is broader, and he might talk about who calls him or provides hard copy or e-mail requests.
"How do your coworkers create purchase orders?" Issue: This is confusing and sounds like a trap.	"Is there another way to create a purchase order?"

- Role of person and primary responsibilities

- Open-ended questions

- Space for answers

- Space for interviewers' insights

- Action item box for flagging key pieces of information as a business requirement, user requirement, supplemental requirement, new requirements risk, assumption, or constraint.

+ Conduct the interview:

- With senior management, the challenge is ensuring that the individual has the expertise or formal position to speak for the organization. In matrix organizations, many directors are not able to make commitments for the organization. Ask the person if she can speak for the entire organization or if it is appropriate to also gather information from others.

- For all user categories, work with two or three users to get a comprehensive picture.

- Create a thank-you script stating that you appreciate the person's time and involvement and stating how the person's involvement will help in creating high-quality requirements.

- Create a follow-up script telling the person how the information will be used, whether it will be held confidential, and the next steps for follow-up or project involvement.

+ Use two interviewers, one to ask questions and one to document results.

+ Allow time in the schedule for both of the interviewers to debrief and document the interview results immediately after the interview is over, while information and impressions are still clear in their minds.

> One of the biggest challenges in elicitation is figuring out the best questions to ask.

Sample Questions

Functional Requirements Questions
What are other ways to accomplish this goal?
Tell me about your frustrations with this process.
What makes a good day? A bad day?
If you could wave a wand and make it different, what would the process look like?
Nonfunctional Requirements Questions
What standards or regulations should we be aware of?
Usability Questions
Who is going to use the product or process?
What purpose is accomplished by using the product or process?
What equipment, tools, templates, and inputs do people need to use it?
How long should tasks take?
How do you define success?
Intrusion and Detection Prevention Questions
What are actions you take to detect unauthorized system access?
What could be done to prevent improper system access?
Interface Questions
What people do you share information with?
What information is passed to other systems?
Software Attributes Ranking Questions
Safety: How do you plan for safety considerations?
Robustness: What fault tolerance systems are important to you?
Supportability: What failures cause the organization the most pain?
Maintainability: What unexpected system behavior has surprised you?
Operations and Maintenance Questions
Are there things in the operational environment that I should be aware of?
End-of Interview Questions
What didn't I ask that I should have?
Was this interview effective?
If we could change only one thing about the process, what should it be?

Tailoring Requirements Elicitation Interviews

Interviews are necessary and valuable for any type of project. The business analyst scales interview activities to the project environment. Table 9-3 shows interview variances scaled to the project profile.

Table 9-3—Interviews Scaled to Project Size, Risk, Complexity

| Elicitation Technique | Project Profile | | |
	Small Independent Low Risk	Medium Moderately Complex Some Risk	Large Highly Complex Significant Risk
Interview	Can be handled through informal discussions with users	Formal interview sessions with key stakeholders to produce predetermined deliverables	Formal focus group interview sessions with key stakeholder groups, with budgets and timelines for securing stakeholder approval on project deliverables

Chapter 10

Surveys

In This Chapter:

- Types of Requirements Elicitation Surveys

- Benefits of Requirements Elicitation Surveys

- Rules for Effective Requirements Elicitation Surveys

- Tailoring Requirements Elicitation Surveys

A *survey* is a process for quickly gathering information without any type of verification. The term *survey* can also be used to describe an activity such as a review of customer support problems or product failure data. This information is already available to the organization and simply needs to be analyzed. Surveys that gather information without verification are used to:

- Understand the process undergoing change.

- Identify significant areas warranting future study or analysis.

- Obtain information to help determine the appropriate requirements elicitation and analysis activities.

Types of Requirements Elicitation Surveys

A well-crafted survey asks questions in a variety of ways. As with interview questions, there are two basic types of survey questions from which to choose, open-ended and closed-ended.

- *Open-ended questions* do not have one right answer, but rather give respondents an opportunity to answer in their own words. While the responses to open-ended questions can be quite useful, they are more difficult to interpret and catalogue.

- *Closed-ended questions* have a finite set of answers for the respondent to select. Closed-ended questions are easy to standardize and the data lends itself to statistical analysis. Closed-ended questions are difficult to formulate so that all possible answers are provided. To get around this, there is often a choice labeled "Other." If a respondent chooses this option, it is helpful to provide space for an explanation. There are several types of closed-ended questions:

  - Likert scale allows for a ranking from "not very important" to "extremely important" or from "strongly disagree" to "strongly agree."

  - Multiple choice allows the respondents to select the best answer from among possible options.

  - Ordinal asks the respondent to rank order a list of items.

  - Categorical allows the respondent to select a category.

  - Numerical asks for a real number for the answer.

Benefits of Requirements Elicitation Surveys

Surveys are administered to groups of stakeholders to determine information about customers, work practices, and attitudes. Responses are analyzed for functional and supplemental requirements and stakeholder interests and positions. Surveys are particularly valuable when customers are dispersed or employees are in multiple locations. Table 10-1 shows the benefits versus the disadvantages of surveys.

Table 10-1—Benefits versus Disadvantages of Surveys

Benefits of Surveys	Disadvantages of Surveys
• Require limited stakeholders' time • Effective at reaching geographically dispersed stakeholders • Scalable for large audiences • Relatively fast and inexpensive to administer • Supplement more subjective information, such as opinions gained through interviews	• Relatively low response rate • Incentives for responding might be expensive • Use of open-ended questions requires more analysis by the business analyst • Require both instrument training and problem or business domain experience • Poorly worded questions may provide inaccurate information

Rules for Effective Requirements Elicitation Surveys

The business analyst should keep several rules in mind when conducting surveys:

+ Understand what information is needed from the survey respondents. For example:

  □ Focus on the high-priority risks that have been identified in early project meetings or interviews, and write questions to confirm the probability or impact of the risk event or issue.

  □ Identify user satisfaction levels with the existing systems to create a baseline for improvements.

+ Create clear and concise questions. Constructing a valid survey instrument is challenging. Strive to:

  □ Be direct. "How many hours do you use the system" versus "How often do you use the system?"

- Be unambiguous. "Rate yourself as being a novice, an average user, or an expert user of the system" versus "Do you consider yourself to be an expert?"

- Save complex questions for later in the survey. "In the space below, provide additional information about how the system could improve the processing of exempt payroll."

- Save demographic information—age group, role, division, gender—for last to avoid feelings that this is a personal reflection.

+ Create rewards for participating. For example:

  - Provide visibility for the division or department with the highest percentage of responses.

  - Consider a monetary incentive or reward a random participant with a voucher for a night on the town.

+ Create the survey using the inexpensive online tools that are readily available. It is increasingly easy and cost-effective to develop surveys online and to create an anonymous portal that calculates results.

+ Notify the participants when the survey is available and continue to remind them to participate.

+ Analyze the survey results. This is the hardest part. There may be some poorly performing questions due to ambiguity or confusion or even errors in the survey instrument itself.

Tailoring Requirements Elicitation Surveys

Surveys can be valuable for most projects. The business analyst scales survey activities to the project environment. Table 10-2 shows interview variances scaled to the project profile.

Table 10-2—Surveys Scaled to Project Size, Risk, Complexity

Elicitation Technique	Project Profile		
	Small Independent Low Risk	Medium Moderately Complex Some Risk	Large Highly Complex Significant Risk
Surveys	Not necessary if stakeholders know each other, the business, and the technical domain	Useful—User surveys can quickly gather information or measure current state user satisfaction or needs	Always—User surveys are needed to measure current state user satisfaction or needs and validate stakeholder assessments

Chapter 11

Documentation Review

In This Chapter:

- Benefits of Documentation Reviews
- Rules for Effective Documentation Reviews
- Tailoring Documentation Reviews

Benefits of Documentation Reviews

A considerable amount of information about the business requirements can be gleaned by reviewing existing business rules, regulations, policies, user guides, contractual documentation, prior project archives, and lessons learned. Table 11-1 shows the benefits versus the disadvantages of documentation reviews. Usually a review of the existing business process area documentation is completed to help create the context for understanding the scope of project work.

Rules for Effective Requirements Documentation Reviews

The business analyst should keep in mind several rules when conducting documentation reviews:

- Know the purpose for reviewing. As with other activities, this task is managed and time-bound to ensure effective use of

Table 11-1—Benefits versus Disadvantages
of Documentation Reviews

Benefits of Documentation Review	Disadvantages of Documentation Review
• Current process documentation provides a starting point	• Existing documents may be old and out-of-date • The reviewer needs domain and technical expertise to determine if existing documentation reflects actual practices • Can be time consuming, and may not provide the desired payback

project resources. Potential documentation review purposes include:

▫ Prior system implementations can be reviewed for functional and supplemental requirements. This can help structure the current business requirements documentation into as-is sections and incremental to-be sections.

▫ Technical documentation is reviewed for high-level solution architecture, business rules, and test scenarios.

▫ Lessons learned are reviewed to capture those golden nuggets of information regarding what went right and wrong on previous projects.

• Begin to create the rough draft outline of the business requirements document and fill in the relevant sections with the information that is collected through the review.

▫ Populate the glossary with terms from former project documentation.

▫ Add existing system documentation references and locations to the appendix.

Tailoring Documentation Reviews

Documentation reviews can be valuable for most projects. The business analyst scales activities to the project environment. Table 11-2 shows document review variances scaled to the project profile.

Table 11-2—Document Reviews Scaled to Project Size, Risk, Complexity

Elicitation Technique	Project Profile		
	Small Independent Low Risk	Medium Moderately Complex Some Risk	Large Highly Complex Significant Risk
Documentation Reviews	Required	Required	Required

Chapter 12

Analyzing Interfaces

In This Chapter:

- Benefits of Interface Analysis
- Types of Interface Analysis Meetings
- Rules for Effective Interface Analysis
- Tailoring Interface Analysis

Analyzing interfaces involves reviewing the system, people, and process linkages that will exist in the proposed business solution. System interfaces define system interactions: which systems provide input, which systems require output, and what medium is used. Interface analysis can also describe what manual or automated processes the proposed business solution requires.

Benefits of Interface Analysis

Analyzing interfaces enables the creation of a list of inputs and outputs that other systems, processes, or people will use. Table 12-1 shows benefits and disadvantages of interface analysis.

Types of Interface Analysis Meetings

Common interface analysis meeting types are:

- **Customer review meetings.** Formal requirements are identified that provide the linkages between information, people, processes, and systems that are necessary to provide a robust, complete, and accurate solution.

+ **Developer review meetings.** Early, high-level requirements documentation and system models are reviewed to identify interfaces, regulations, or technical standards.

Table 12-1—Benefits and Disadvantages of Interface Analysis

Benefits of Analyzing Interfaces	Disadvantages of Analyzing Interfaces
+ Discovers missed interfaces and their purpose + Determines regulations or interface standards + Provides missed requirements + Uncovers areas of project risk	+ Not useful as a standalone elicitation activity if domain and technical expertise is high + Can begin to focus on too many technical details + Can be redundant with modeling activities

Rules for Effective Interface Analysis

Key rules for effective interface analysis are:

+ Conduct an internal meeting as a part of any product development process. At this meeting, developers can take an honest and early first look at the system to see inconsistencies and errors.

+ Create clearly defined roles for follow-up:

  □ Have the project manager clarify scope boundary issues with the sponsor or the group that is paying for the project.

  □ Have the business analyst follow up on open issues on user intention and goals.

+ Continue to update business requirements documents with information and assumptions about interfaces. The documentation may be in the form of a list or updated use case diagrams or context diagrams.

Tailoring Interface Analysis

Interface analysis is necessary and valuable for any initiative size. The business analyst scales activities to the project environment. Table 12-2 shows the variances scaled to the project profile.

Table 12-2—Interface Analysis Scaled to Project Size, Risk, Complexity

Elicitation Technique	Project Profile		
	Small Independent Low Risk	Medium Moderately Complex Some Risk	Large Highly Complex Significant Risk
Interface Analysis	As needed if technical or business knowledge is high	Always needed to ensure complete understanding of business events	Always needed to ensure business understanding of users and technical understanding of architecture

Chapter 13

Eliciting Supplemental Requirements

In This Chapter:

- Benefits of Eliciting Supplemental Requirements
- Rules for Effective Elicitation of Supplemental Requirements
- Tailoring Supplemental Requirements Elicitation

Eliciting supplemental requirements involves compiling a list of solution-quality expectations. These expectations impose constraints on the requirements.

Benefits of Eliciting Supplemental Requirements

Table 13-1 shows the benefits versus the disadvantages of eliciting supplemental requirements.

Many organizations have standards for drafting supplemental requirements. If standards do not exist, the business analyst will need to create them for the project level. If the performing organization has standards for drafting supplemental requirements, the business analyst only documents exceptions to the standards that the project will follow.

Table 13-1—Benefits versus Disadvantages of Eliciting Supplemental Requirements

Benefits of Eliciting Supplemental Requirements	Disadvantages of Eliciting Supplemental Requirements
• Uncovers business requirements, user requirements, and performance requirements that have been missed • Improves requirements coverage early in the process • Uncovers areas of end-user/customer solution adoption risk	• It can be difficult for end-users to articulate quality specifications without prototypes so they can visualize the proposed business solution

Rules for Effective Elicitation of Supplemental Requirements

Key rules for effective supplemental requirements reviews are:

+ Document the source of supplemental requirements. Resources change quickly and documenting the source will improve stability of requirements.

+ Supplemental requirements are also formal requirements, and should be reviewed and approved by key stakeholders.

Tailoring Supplemental Requirements

Eliciting supplemental requirements is necessary and valuable for any initiative size. The business analyst scales activities to the project environment. Table 13-2 shows the variances scaled to the project profile.

Table 13-2—Supplemental Requirements Elicitation Scaled to Project Size, Risk, Complexity

Elicitation Technique	Project Profile		
	Small Independent Low Risk	Medium Moderately Complex Some Risk	Large Highly Complex Significant Risk
Elicit Supplemental Requirements	Always needed; combine with documentation reviews and interface analysis	Internal meetings with developers to review early elicitation results for exceptions to existing supplemental requirements standards	Conduct separate meetings for supplemental reviews with the technical resources responsible for developing or testing to those standards

Summary

+ Effective requirements are the best defense against requirements risks to projects. Since defective requirements contribute significantly to project cost and schedule overruns, professional business analysts are focusing heavily on requirements planning and elicitation. Use another volume in this series, *Getting It Right: Business Requirement Analysis Tools and Techniques*, to hone your requirements analysis, specification, documentation, and validation skills.

+ The key elicitation activities are brainstorming, discovery sessions, interviews, surveys, documentation reviews, interface analysis, and supplemental requirements analysis.

+ Brainstorming is the process of generating ideas and then gaining consensus on which ideas to go forward with for additional action. Its strength is that it produces creative results, and its weakness is that it introduces assumptions too early.

+ Workshop and discovery sessions are formal meetings with multiple stakeholders. The purpose of the meetings is documenting requirements.

+ Interviewing is a systematic process of collecting information from sponsors, customers, and users. A formal script enables consistent interpretation of results.

+ Surveys are the administration of a written set of questions to the stakeholders. Surveys reduce the time commitment required from the stakeholder groups. Incentives are often required to improve the low response rate.

+ Documentation reviews are accomplished by reviewing existing system, business policy, and contractual documentation to quickly gain familiarity with the current environment. However, the documentation may be outdated and may not actually reflect the current practices or system.

+ Analyzing interfaces means reviewing the system, people, and process linkages. Use of this technique can uncover missed interfaces or users.

+ Documenting supplemental requirements is a review of the users' expectations of system behavior that may constrain the development of the solution. The process of documenting supplemental requirements also uncovers missed business, user, or supplemental requirements and often requires some prototyping for effective communication with the users.

Action Plan for the Business Analyst

+ Review the common techniques that you use on your current projects.

+ Use additional techniques that are appropriate to project size, complexity, and risk.

+ Utilize a survey to understand how satisfied users are with elicitation results.

+ Compose an interview to ask the project sponsor his or her opinion of the role of the business analyst.

- Include the solution development team in the process of deciding which elicitation techniques should be used on your next project.

Appendixes

Appendix A:
Sample Business Requirements Document

Appendix B:
Sample Business Requirements
Document—Use Cases

Appendix C:
Sample Requirements Management Plan

Appendix A

Sample Business Requirements Document

Logo

Organization Name

Project Title

Business Requirements Document (BRD)

Draft Version: 1.0

Date Prepared:

Prepared by:

Contents

Document Information. 3

Approval 4

1.0 Introduction 5

2.0 Project Stakeholders 6

3.0 Overall Description 6

4.0 User Summary 8

5.0 Functional Requirements 10

6.0 Supplemental Requirements 12

Appendix A: Glossary. 14

Appendix B: Use Cases. 16

Appendix C: Business Solution Cost Estimating 18

Document Information

Revision History

Version	Date	Author(s)	Revision Notes

Approval

The signatures below confirm that this document has been reviewed and is complete and accurate for the project.

Senior Management and Project Team Leads	Signature	Date
		Date
		Date
		Date
		Date
		Date
		Date
		Date

1.0 Introduction

Purpose

Describe the project scope and the phase to which this project applies.

This business requirements document (BRD) describes the functional requirements for release 1.0 of the (insert solution, system or project name here). This document is for use by the members of the project team that will design, construct and verify the system or process. If a feature is included, it is assumed to be of high priority and included in this release.

Project Scope

Provide an overview of the organization or project-level standards, guidelines and expectations.

The (insert solution, system or project name here) will provide (organization name) with the following business and high level feature requirements. Describe the solution in textual terms.

Project Client

Provide the name of the sponsor or the client.

Provide the funding source and name. Describe any background information on the project approval or release of funds to the project.

Project Budget

Provide an overview of the budget constraints and the source of the constraint.

The budget for this system is not to exceed $x, including hardware, software capital equipment, expensed equipment or license purchases.

Project Schedule

Provide an overview of the schedule constraints and the source of the constraints.

The system must be complete within (*insert constraint here*) months but does not need to include all the (*list follow-up phase features or lower priority features here*).

Related Documents

List all documents that exist relating to this project, such as: program documents, document and model templates, defect checklists, glossaries, and standard operating procedures/work instructions.

Examples:
1. Business Case Location or URL
2. Charter Location or URL
3. Supplemental Business Requirements Location or URL
4. Use Cases Location or URL

2.0 Project Stakeholders

Stakeholder Summary

List the stakeholder analysis completed by the business analyst. Identify how representative stakeholders were involved in the requirements discovery (pre-project) process. State how conflicts in stakeholder group interests were resolved.

3.0 Overall Description

Business Need

This describes a high-level summary of the reason that this project was undertaken and the phase to which this project applies (if applicable). State in natural (non-technical) language. The intended audience is either the customer or senior management.

The (*insert solution, system or project name here*) is a new system or process that replaces the current manual processes for (*continue to provide a high-level business overview of the need*).

Business Solution Overview/Problem Domain Model or Business Process Model

This provides a high-level summary of the business solution described in this document. The intended audience is either the customer or senior management. It may be necessary to provide a graphical representation of a high-level business solution describing system boundaries or major components. Provide a textual description of the major components of the system. An example is a context diagram which represents the scope of a business solution at a high level. It identifies actors and events outside the system that interact with it, without describing internal structure. A problem domain model may look like the following:

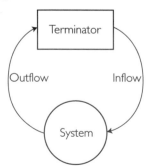

Approaches

State the recommended and alternative approaches to solve the business need. The intended audience is either the customer or senior management.

-
-

Metrics

Discuss the business metrics that will be improved by the solution in specific and measurable terms.

-
-

Assumptions

Project assumptions clarify gray areas in the project scope. List any known assumptions or special requirements that have been made regarding the project that may influence this agreement. Assumptions are made to fill knowledge gaps; they may later prove to be incorrect and can have a significant impact on the project.

-
-

Constraints

Any known constraints imposed by the environment or by management should be noted. Typical constraints may include: fixed budget,

> *limited resources, imposed interim and/or end dates, predetermined software systems and packages and other predetermined solutions.*
>
> ◆
>
> ◆

4.0 User Summary

User Summary

Provide the user analysis completed by the business analyst. Identify how representative users were involved in the requirements discovery process. State how conflicts in user needs were resolved.

Users of the Product/Process

List the user names, roles and their domain knowledge expertise and their technology experience. Describe any other relevant information that impacts requirements. List the prioritization of the users groups. List the user participation in the requirements elicitation, analysis, specification, validation and documentation processes.

User Environment

Describe how the user environment impacts the requirements.

User Classes and Goals

Insert the completed table here. This provides additional information on the high-level commitments made in the use case inventory listed above.

Figure 4-1—Classes

Entities		Method (Behavior)
Donor	1	Give Donation
	2	
	3	
	4	
	5	
	6	
	7	
	8	
	9	
	10	

Constraints, assumptions and dependencies

List all business, product line or technical assumptions and constraints for the requirements life cycle process.

Assumptions

Project assumptions clarify gray areas in the project scope. Any known assumptions that have been made regarding the project that may influence this agreement should be noted in the table below. Assumptions are made to fill knowledge gaps; they may later prove to be incorrect and can have a significant impact on the project.

-
-

Business Constraints

Any known constraints imposed by the environment or by management should be noted. Typical constraints may include: fixed budget, limited resources, imposed interim and/or end dates, predetermined software systems and packages and other predetermined solutions

+

+

Required Design Constraints

+

+

5.0 Functional Requirements

Overview

Describe the project scope and the phase to which this project applies.

The (insert solution, system or project name) is a new system that replaces the current manual processes. An example is provided below.

5.1 Fundraising Tracking System (FTS)

5.1.1 General Requirements

1. Assumption: FTS only allows a donation to be entered by an internal user. There is no capability to provide this function via the web in the 1st release of the product.
2. Donor, gift and corporate grants business rules are described in *supplemental* section
3. The system shall have a configurable gift eligibility table of:
   a. Gift offering programs
   b. Marketing scripts
   c. Assumption: This table will be maintained by IT. Business tool owners may open support cases to ask IT to implement changes requested by marketing.
4. The system shall display the following screen elements for each donor (pending UE review):
   a. Donor Name
   b. Donor Address
   c. Previous donation history
   d. Previous gift history

5.1.2 Give Donations

1. The system shall display the following non-editable screen elements for each donor (pending UE review):
   a. Donor name
      i. First name
      ii. Last name
      iii. Middle initial
      iv. Salutations
      v. Name of spouse
      vi. Any credentials
   b. Donor address
      i. Street
      ii. 2nd Street
      iii. City
      iv. State
      v. Zip Code
   c. Email address
   d. Types of donation payment options
   e. Donation amount
      i. Single donation
      ii. Donation amount by month
         1. Start date of donation
         2. End date of donation
2. The system shall review the entered donor information and:
   a. Confirm there is a record

5.1.3 Register for email newsletter (TBD)

5.1.4 Create, View, Modify and Delete Marketing Content (TBD)

Risks

Any future events that if they occur will positively or negatively impact the project.

+

+

Open and Closed Issues

Item	Date	Who Raised Issue?	Urgency	Description of Issue or Action Item	Closed	Comments
1						
2						
3						

6.0 Supplemental Requirements

Describe the supplemental requirements required by the users.

The following are sample supplemental requirements.

1. **Access Management Requirements**
1.1. **Roles and Permissions**
    1.1.1. Describe, at a conceptual level, who will have access to the system or its components and what type of access they will have

1.2. **System Impacts**

2. **External Interface Requirements**
2.1. **Usability Requirements**
    2.1.1. The Fundraising Tracking System will provide help links to explain usage of each page.
    2.1.2. Wireframes (available before requirements phase exit)
    2.1.3. Field-level descriptions (available in design phase)

2.2. **Hardware Interfaces**
    2.2.1. TBD

2.3. **Software Interfaces**
    2.3.1. The Assistance Inc. accounting systems
    2.3.1.1. To allow a phone rep to check whether there is a record for a donor on file
    2.3.1.2. To transit new donor name and address information
    2.3.1.3. To update donor name and address information
    2.3.1.4. To transmit the donation amount
    2.3.1.5. To change or cancel the donation amount

2.4 Communications Interfaces

2.4.1. The FTS shall send shipping an email message to send a gift to a donor

2.4.2. The FTS shall send donor an email message to a donor for a donation commitment

2.4.3. The FTS shall send donor an email message to a donor for a donation acknowledge and details of the donation payment.

2.4.4. The FTS shall send donor an email message for a donation payment failure.

3. Security Requirements

3.1. Specify in business language the security or privacy constraints that the system must respect or adhere to.

4. Performance Requirements

4.1. State in business terms user or system requirements that designers need to consider.

5. Software Quality Attributes

5.1. State the product quality characteristics that are important to stakeholders. Some to consider are maintainability, supportability, interoperability, availability (if not covered under performance).

6. Business Rules

6.1. An agreed-upon procedure, guideline, regulation or standard that leads to a decision on how a system should respond to a condition. Business rules document the policies that the business must follow. These rules may be documented as text, or created as a matrix of conditions and business solution responses. These are not functional requirements in themselves, but they may require functional requirements to execute the rules.

Appendix A: Glossary

Key requirements terms

Define key requirements terms and acronyms

- ✦
- ✦

Appendix B: Use Cases

List other models created during the requirements process.

Appendix C: Business Solution Cost Estimating

Project Hardware

Describe the hardware that is available or needs to be purchased for the project development. Describe what networks are available for possible use for the project. If the hardware platform is to be purchased then a technical architecture describing what is necessary should be documented.

Project Software

Describe the application and system software that is available or needs to be purchased for the project development.

Operations Impact

Describe at a high-level the hardware and software required for operational locations at which the application will be used. Provide assumptions for hardware/software, cabling, and connectivity purchases. Describe headcount required to administer or operate the hardware/software purchased.

Business Operations Impact

Describe at a high-level the resources, facilities, training, desktop tools, servers, printers, etc. required for operational locations at which the application will be used. Describe the organizational requirements (new organizational structures, new capabilities, training, etc.) to operate business solution.

Sample Business Requirements Document—Use Cases

Logo

Organization Name

Project Title

Business Requirements Document (BRD)

Draft Version: 1.0

Date Prepared:

Prepared by:

Contents

Document Information. 3

Approval 4

1.0 Introduction 5

2.0 Project Stakeholders 6

3.0 Overall Description 6

4.0 User Summary 8

5.0 Functional Requirements .9

6.0 Supplemental Requirements 11

Appendix A: Glossary. 12

Appendix B: Use Cases. 12

Appendix C: Business Solution Cost Estimating 14

Document Information

Revision History

Version	Date	Author(s)	Revision Notes

Approval

The signatures below confirm that this document has been reviewed and is complete and accurate for the project.

Senior Management and Project Team Leads	Signature	Date
		Date
		Date
		Date
		Date
		Date
		Date
		Date

1.0 Introduction

Purpose

Describe the project scope and the phase to which this project applies.

This business requirements document (BRD) describes the requirements for release 1.0 of the (*insert solution, system or project name here*). This document is for use by the members of the project team that will design, construct and verify the system or process and by the customer to confirm that this solution will satisfy their needs.

Project Scope

Provide an overview of the organization or project standards, guidelines and expectations.

The (*insert solution, system or project name here*) will provide (*organization name*) with the following business and high level feature requirements. This document represents the scope of the project. If a feature is included, it is assumed to be of high priority and included in this release.

Describe the solution in high-level textual terms.

Project Client

Provide the name of the sponsor or the client.

Provide the funding source and name. Describe any background information on the project approval or release of funds to the project.

Project Budget

Provide an overview of the budget constraints and the source of the constraint.

The budget for this system is not to exceed ($x), including hardware, software capital equipment, expensed equipment or license purchases.

Project Schedule

Provide an overview of the schedule constraints and the source of the constraints.

The system must be complete within (*insert constraint here*) months but does not need to include all the (*list follow-up phase features or lower priority features here*).

Related Documents

List all documents that exist relating to this project, such as: program documents, document and model templates, defect checklists, glossaries, and standard operating procedures/work instructions. Also list any current system document that was used to describe the as-is process or was used in re-engineering solutions.

Examples:
1. Business Case (Location or URL)
2. Charter (Location or URL)
3. Supplemental Business Requirements (Location or URL)
4. Use Cases (Location or URL)

2.0 Project Stakeholders

Stakeholder Summary

List the results of the stakeholder analysis completed by the project manager. Identify how representative stakeholders were involved in the requirements discovery (pre-project) process. State how conflicts in stakeholder group interests were resolved.

3.0 Overall Description

Business Need

This describes a high- level summary if the reason that this project was undertaken and the phase to which this project applies (if applicable). Use natural, non-technical language. The intended audience is either the customer or senior management.

The (*insert solution, system or project name here*) is a new system or process that replaces the current manual processes for (*continue to provide a high-level business overview of the need*).

Business Solution Overview/Problem Domain Model or Business Process Model

This provides a high-level summary of the business solution described in this document. The intended audience is either the customer or senior management. It may be necessary to provide a graphical representation of a high-level business solution describing system boundaries or major components. Give a description of the major components of the system.

An example is a use case diagram serving as the problem domain model. This represents scope of the business solution at a high level. It identifies actors and events outside the system that interact with it, without describing internal structure. A problem domain model may look like the following:

Figure 3-1—Use Case Diagram

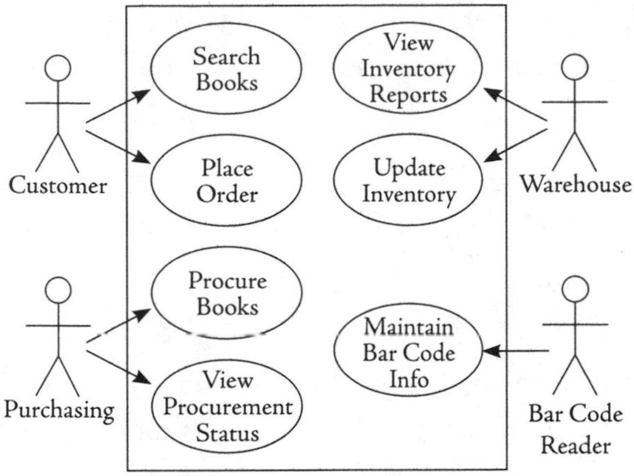

The summary may also be stated in a matrix

Figure 3-2—Use Case Inventory

Name of Use Case
Search Books
View Inventory Reports
Place Order
Update Inventory
Procure Books
Maintain Bar Code Info
View Procurement Sales

Approaches

State the recommended and alternative approaches to solve the business need. The intended audience is either the customer or senior management.

   ◆

   ◆

Metrics

Discuss the business metrics that will be improved by the implementation of the solution in specific and measurable terms.

- ◆

- ◆

Assumptions

Project assumptions clarify gray areas in the project. List any known assumptions or special requirements that have been made regarding the project that may influence this agreement should be noted in the table below. Assumptions are made to fill knowledge gaps; they may later prove to be incorrect and can have a significant impact on the project.

- ◆

- ◆

Constraints

Any known constraints imposed by the environment or by management should be noted. Typical constraints may include: fixed budget, limited resources, imposed interim and/or end dates, predetermined software systems and packages and other predetermined solutions

- ◆

- ◆

4.0 User Summary

User Summary

Provide the user analysis completed by the business analyst. Identify how representative users were involved in the requirements discovery process. State how conflicts in user needs were resolved.

Users of the Product/Process

List the user names, roles and their domain knowledge expertise and their technology experience. Describe any other relevant information that impacts requirements. List the prioritization of the users groups. List the user participation in the requirements elicitation, analysis, specification, validation and documentation processes.

User environment

Describe how the user environment impacts the requirements.

User Classes and Goals

Insert the completed table here. This provides additional information on the high-level commitments made in the use case inventory listed above.

Figure 4-1—Actor Goals

Primary Actor/User		Use Case Goals/Feature Goals
Donor	1	Give Donation
	2	
	3	
	4	
	5	
	6	
	7	
	8	
	9	
	10	

5.0 Functional Requirements

Feature Description

Describe the business solution behavior requested by the users.

The following are sample business scenarios that are included in the first release of the Donation Tracking system.

1.1. Give donations

1.1.1. As-Is

An individual donation is either received over the phone or in the mail. This information is written down on a donor form if received over the phone. Only actual donation information is entered into the accounting system. Fields are not verified for accuracy.

1.1.2. To-Be Description and Priority

An individual donor who is verified to have information listed in the Fundraising Tracking System will be able to provide payment information. An individual donor may change the donation amount, change the donation payment method or cancel their donation. This must be in the first release of the project.

1.1.3. To-Be Stimulus/Response Sequences

Stimulus: Donor agrees to provide a donation
Response: Phone rep asks donor for details of the payment

Stimulus: Donor requests a change in donation amount
Response: If donation amount is found, system allows phone rep to modify a previous donation amount.

Stimulus:	Donor requests a cancellation of a donation amount
Response:	If donation amount is found, system allows phone rep to cancel a previous donation amount.

1.1.4. To-Be Give Donations Functional Requirements

Donation.Place:	The system will let a phone rep who is logged into the Fundraising Tracking System enter one or more donations
Donation.Place.Record:	The system shall confirm that the donor is has an information record in the system.
Donation.Place.Record.No:	If the donor is not listed in the system, the system will collect the information needed to continue with the donation process.
Donation.Place.Date:	The system shall prompt the phone rep for the donation date.
Donation.Gift.Select:	The system shall prompt the phone rep to offer gifts to donors (see BR**)
Donation.Pay.Methods:	When the donor is done providing donations and selecting a gift, the system shall ask for a payment method.

Donation.Done:	When the donor has confirmed the donation, the system shall do the following as a single transaction:
Donation:Done:Store:	Assign the next available donation number to the donation with an initial status of "accepted."
Donation:Done:Ship:	Send a message to the shipping clerk to send the selected gift.
Donation:Done:Donor:	Send a message to the Patron with the donation number and the payment information.
Donation:Done:Accounting:	Send a message to the accounting system with the donation information.
Donation:Done:Failure:	If any step of the Donation.Done fails, the system shall roll back the transaction and notify the donor that the donation payment was unsuccessful, along with the reason for the failure.

(Functional requirements for changing and canceling donations are not provided in this example.)

1.2. **Register for email newsletter**
TBD

1.3. **Create, View, Modify and Delete Marketing Content**
TBD

1.4. **Report Requirements (Ad hoc and Scheduled)**
TBD

Risks

Any future events that if they occur will positively or negatively impact the project.

+

+

Open and Closed Issues

Item	Date	Who Raised Issue?	Urgency	Description of Issue or Action Item	Closed	Comments
1						
2						
3						

6.0 Supplemental Requirements

Describe the supplemental requirements required by the users.

The following are sample supplemental requirements.

1. **Access Management Requirements**
1.1. **Roles and Permissions**

    1.1.1. Describe, at a conceptual level, who will have access to the system or its components and what type of access they will have

1.2. **System Impacts**

2. **External Interface Requirements**
2.1. **Usability Requirements**

    2.1.1. The Fundraising Tracking System will provide help links to explain usage of each page.

    2.1.2. Wireframes (available before requirements phase exit)

    2.1.3. Field-level descriptions (available in design phase)

2.2. **Hardware Interfaces**

    2.2.1. TBD

2.3. **Software Interfaces**

    2.3.1. The Assistance Inc. accounting systems

    2.3.1.1. To allow a phone rep to check whether there is a record for a donor on file

    2.3.1.2. To transit new donor name and address information

    2.3.1.3. To update donor name and address information

    2.3.1.4. To transmit the donation amount

    2.3.1.5. To change or cancel the donation amount

2.4 Communications Interfaces

2.4.1. The FTS shall send shipping an email message to send a gift to a donor

2.4.2. The FTS shall send donor an email message to a donor for a donation commitment

2.4.3. The FTS shall send donor an email message to a donor for a donation acknowledge and details of the donation payment.

2.4.4. The FTS shall send donor an email message for a donation payment failure.

3. Security Requirements

3.1. Specify in business language the security or privacy constraints that the system must respect or adhere to.

4. Performance Requirements

4.1. State in business terms user or system requirements that designers need to consider.

5. Software Quality Attributes

5.1. State the product quality characteristics that are important to stakeholders. Some to consider are maintainability, supportability, interoperability, availability (if not covered under performance).

6. Business Rules

6.1. An agreed-upon procedure, guideline, regulation or standard that leads to a decision on how a system should to respond to a condition. Business rules document the policies that the business must follow. These rules may be documented as text, or created as a matrix of conditions and business solution responses. These are not functional requirements in themselves, but they may require functional requirements to execute the rules.

Appendix A: Glossary

Key requirements terms

Defines key requirements terms and acronyms

- ◆

- ◆

Appendix B: Use Cases

List high-level use case information (further information will be provided in the requirements phase as each iteration of the use cases are completed).

Case #	Feature	Business Requirement	Actors	Pre-Condition	Post-Condition
1	Give Donation				
2	Change Donation				
3	Cancel Donation				

A sample use case is provided below.

B-1 Give Donation

1. Description

An internal user enters information provided by a donor into the Fundraising Tracking System (FTS).

2. Actors

1. FTS Users
2. FTS
3. Security Management (SM) API

3. Pre-conditions

1. Donor has an existing record
2. User access to FTS Give Donation function in SM API

4. Basic Flow

Step	Description
1	The use case begins when a user wants to enter donation information
2	The user logs in.
3	The system grants access to the Donations screen according the permissions on SM matrix.
4	The system searches for donor information *(Alt Course A: Can not find existing donor* *(Alt Course B: New Donor*
5	The system excludes donors that are corporate grant partners.
6	The system displays a list of eligible last names, their first names and address *(Exception Course A: Corporate donors are not displayed)*
7	User selects the displayed user that matches information provided by the donor. *(Exception Course B: Donor chooses not to continue with the donation process)*
8	The system displays the new donation form and the user enters the information.
9	The use case ends when the user has entered donation information

5. Alternative Flow

Step	Description
Alt A	The system searches for donor information
4	The system can not find any donor information. User can navigate back to the initial donations screen to enter alternative spellings.
Alt B	The user creates a new donor record
4	The system allows the user to enter new donor information.

6. Exception Flow

Step	Description
Exp A	The system displays a list of eligible last names, their first names and address
6	The system excludes corporate grant donors
Exp B	User selects the displayed user that matches information provided by the donor.
7	The donor or user chooses to exit the transaction. Information is not saved.

7. Post-conditions

1. Successful transaction screen displayed
2. Donation posted to accounting
3. Credit card charged

Appendix C: Business Solution Cost Estimating

Project Hardware

Describe the hardware that is available or needs to be purchased for the project development. Describe what networks are available for possible use for the project. If the hardware platform is to be purchased then a technical architecture describing what is necessary should be documented.

Project Software

Describe the application and system software that is available or needs to be purchased for the project development.

IT Operations Impact

Describe at a high-level the hardware and software required for operational locations at which the application will be used. Provide a assumptions for hardware/software, cabling, and connectivity purchases. Describe headcount required to administer or operate the hardware/software purchased.

Business Operations Impact

Describe at a high-level the resources, facilities, training, desktop tools, servers, printers, etc. required for operational locations at which the application will be used. Describe the organizational requirements (new organizational structures, new capabilities, training, etc.) to operate business solution.

Sample Requirements Management Plan

Logo
Organization Name
Project Title
Requirements Management Plan (RMP)
Draft Version: 1.0
Date Prepared:
Prepared by:

Contents

Document Information. 3

Approval 4

1.0 Introduction 5

2.0 Stakeholders 6

3.0 Users 7

4.0 Requirement Deliverables. 8

5.0 Verification and Validation Processes 10

6.0 Change Management Processes. 11

7.0 Risk Management 12

8.0 Deliverables Owners, Dependencies and Resource
Estimates. 13

9.0 Glossary. 16

Document Information

Revision History

Version	Date	Author(s)	Revision Notes

Approval

The signatures below confirm that this document has been reviewed and is complete and accurate for the project.

Team Member	Signature	
		Date
		Date
		Date
		Date
		Date
		Date
		Date

1.0 Introduction

Overview of Scope

Describe the purpose, scope, and objectives of the document.

This document describes the guidelines used by the project for eliciting, analyzing, specifying, documenting and validating the business requirements. In addition, it describes the process to be used for requirement traceability and change management. This document is a subsidiary element of the overall project plan.

Overview of Requirements Standards

Provide an overview of the organizational standards, how they have been tailored for this project, and any additional project-specific guidelines and expectations.

Related Documents

List all related document, such as: program documents, test plans, glossaries, standard operating procedures/work instructions. For existing documents, provide author, issue date and storage location of the electronic version. Potential examples include:

- Business Case Document [insert author, date and location]

- Business Requirements Document [insert author, date and location]

- Supplementary Requirements Specification [insert author, date and location]

2.0 Stakeholders

List the stakeholders who are involved in the requirements definition and management process.

This is a listing of the stakeholders that will be involved in requirements gathering, documenting and management. This is not an exhaustive project stakeholder analysis, but is meant to provide the preliminary information needed to begin the requirements elicitation activities. It will also contribute to the overall stakeholder analysis completed by the project manager.

Stakeholder Name	Stakeholder Role/Job Title	Description of Why Project Requires Their Input or Knowledge	Degree of Influence	Required Project Involvement

Open Stakeholder Issues:

- *Sample: Lack of agreement on product champion role*

Open Stakeholder Risks:

- *Sample: Lack of access to stakeholders for business requirements*

3.0 Users

List end users who are involved in the requirements management process

This is a listing of the end user groups that will be involved in the project. This is not an exhaustive user stakeholder analysis, but is meant to provide the preliminary information needed to begin the requirements elicitation activities. It will also contribute to the overall stakeholder analysis completed by the project manager.

User Group Name	User Roles	Domain Expertise	Technology Expertise	User Group Priority

Open User Involvement Issues:

- *Sample: Lack of funding to cover all user classes*

Open User Involvement Risks:

- *Sample: Lack of access to users for use case development*

4.0 Requirement Deliverables

4.1 Documents and Models

List the requirement documents, deliverables and other artifacts that will be created by the project team. Examples of requirement artifacts appear below; it is not meant to be an exhaustive list.

The following requirement artifacts are required for this project.

Document Name	Requirements Type(s)	Description
Business requirements document	Functional	Capability desired by the customer.
	Assumptions	Something assumed to be real, true or certain for the project.
	Constraints	A project limitation.
	Glossary	Defines important terms used by project stakeholders. Terms are defined in natural (non-technical) language.
	Design constraints	A design limitation. Content most often provided by the technical design team.
	Business rules	An agreed-upon business procedure that leads to a decision on how to respond to a condition. Content most often provided by customers and users.
Use case and any other usage, process or high-level data model	Functional	Provides high-level view of all Use-Cases and Actors (or indicate elements for each analysis model required) for this release documented in xxx vendor application. Content provided by customers and users
Supplementary requirements document	Supplemental	Provides non-feature related information.
Requirements traceability matrix	Functional	Captures the allocation of functional requirements to system components, e.g., design specifications, program modules, test case, etc.
Design specification	n/a	Contains the design elements and architecture for the proposed business solution.
Test plan	n/a	Contains the strategy for testing coverage within the project.
Test case	n/a	A specific set of test inputs, environmental conditions, and expected results developed for a particular objective.

4.2 Attributes

Separately list the information that is required when specifying requirements. Sample information required appears below; it is not meant to be an exhaustive list.

The following is a list, by requirement type, of the required information that must be captured for each type of artifact.

Requirement Attributes for Functional Requirements

- # (unique identifier)

- Status

- Benefit/business value (quantified or high/medium/low)

- Effort (quantified or high/medium/low)

- Description

- Rationale

- Source

- Event/use case number

- Supporting materials/documents

- Dependencies (required whether manual or automated system)

- Change history (this may be unnecessary if requirements are managed by an automated application)

- Priority (based on business value)

Requirement Attributes for Supplemental Requirements

+ Effort (quantified or high/medium/low)

Requirement Attributes for Actors

+ Name and brief description of role

Requirement Attributes for Use Cases

+ Name

+ Brief description

+ Basic flow

+ Alternate flow

+ Special requirements

+ Pre-condition

+ Post-condition

5.0 Verification and Validation Processes

Allocation Process

Describe the requirement allocation process.

Traceability Process

Describe the requirements traceability process.

Peer Review Process

Describe the peer review process.

Customer Review Process

Describe the process and participants for the customer review process.

Management Review Process

Describe the process and participants for the management review process, including the requirements phase-exit control gate review.

6.0 Change Management Processes

Change Management Process

Describe the requirements change management process.

7.0 Risk Management

Describe the requirement risk identification, assessment, and risk response planning process.

Note: the requirement risk management process is provided to the project manager for further incorporation into the overall project risk management plan.

8.0 Deliverables Owners, Dependencies, and Resource Estimates

Provide project planning detail for all the artifacts to be created to manage requirements. Note: this list should include all deliverables listed in Section 4.0. Examples of requirement artifacts appear below; it is not meant to be an exhaustive list.

The requirements deliverables, ownership, and project planning information are as follows.

Requirements Development Artifacts

Key Deliverables	Owner	Time Est.	Dependency	Template	Comments / Risks / Issues
Requirements Management Plan Document	BA	x hours	Business Case and Charter	RMP.dot	No organizational template exists which could delay approval since there is not agreement on content
Committed Stakeholders	BA/PM	n/a	none	na	Need donor user representative to confirm understanding of the use cases
Elicitation Phase					
Requirements Workshop	BA	24 hours	Approved Requirements Management Plan		Estimate may need to be doubled as we need additional training or facilitation help in this area
Analysis Phase					
Context Diagram	BA	x hours	High-Level Product Description	ContextDiagram.dot	Accounting doesn't want any changes but it is a required interface
User Classes & Goals	BA	x hours	Stakeholder analysis	Usergoals.dot	Need product champions for each user class
Prioritization of Use Cases	BA	x hours	User Classes & Goals	n/a – see User Classes & Goals	
Use Case Diagram	BA	n/a			None – will use User Class list since small number of use cases
Use Case Scenarios	BA	60 hours	UC Diagram	Usecase.dot UCDefectList.dot	The organization has not used these before and so there is training involved
Validation Phase					
Prototypes	TL/BA	60 hours	Use Case Scenarios	n/a	Need a user product champion and a dedicated resource from accounting

Key Deliverables	Owner	Time Est.	Dependency	Template	Comments / Risks / Issues
Feasibility Studies/ Reliability Studies	BA	n/a	Draft BRD		Create an RFP from the BRD to research availability and feature sets of COTS applications
Documentation Phase					
Project Summary	PM	x hours	Business Case and Charter	Charter.dot	Missing charter
Business Requirements Document	BA	n/a	Elicitation & draft Analysis models complete	Yes	Choose to create only Use Cases and Supplementary Business Requirements
Supplemental Business Requirements	BA/SA	24 hours	Draft BRD	SBR.dot SBRDefectList.dot	Organization has not agreed on a template or organizational standards
Glossary	BA	4 hours	Use Case Scenarios	n/a	There isn't an existing glossary so only critical terms will be documented

Requirements Management Artifacts

Key Deliverables	Ownership	Time *	Dependency	Template	Comments / Risks / Issues
Requirements Traceability Matrix	BA/SA	TBD	Decision on tool purchase.	TBD	Will provide time estimate before requirements phase gate
Test Plan	Test Manager/BA	TBD	BRD, Use Cases, Supplement Business Requirements	TBD	Will provide time estimate before requirements phase gate
Requirements Change Management Process	PM/BA	TBD	Decision on tool purchase. PM to create process.	TBD	Will provide time estimate before requirements phase gate

*Note: This may not be the final time estimate for the requirements activities that will be used in the project schedule. TBD indicates tradeoff decisions on which activities to include in the final project schedule.

Environmental Needs and Responsibilities

Provide details of any special environment set-up needs. This section covers office space, equipment needs, and software tool needs. Resources may be available within the organization but need to be identified for scheduling and chargebacks.

The environmental needs for the project are as follows.

Deliverable	Description	Owner

Training

Provide details of training required for all core and extended team members to accomplish the requirement activities.

The training needs for the project are as follows.

Resource Type	Training Need, Timing, and Cost	Functional Manager/Owner Commitments (y/n)

Requirements Schedule

Provide the milestone schedule commitments to be used in overall project planning.

The requirements milestones and schedule for the project are as follows.

Milestone	Due Date

9.0 Glossary

Define key requirements terms to be included in the overall project glossary. Define terms in natural, nontechnical language.

Key requirements terms

+ Key term 1—explanation of term

Index

A

accountable role (RACI model),
34–35
    agile development model
    project life cycle of, 52, 60–62, 66
    workshop sessions, 105–106
assumptions, 8–9

B

brainstorming
    defined, 3, 97
    rules for, 98–99
    stakeholder involvement, 32
    tailoring sessions, 100
    types of, 98
BRD (business requirements
    document), 10–12
BSLC (business solution life cycle), 4.
    See also requirements planning
business outcome, 9
business process improvement,
    104–105
business requirements
    defined, 7–9
    sample document, 139–160
    sample use cases, 161–183
    workshops focusing on, 101–110
business requirements document
    (BRD), 10–12
business rules, 8–9

business solution, 6–7, 82–83
business solution life cycle (BSLC), 4.
    See also requirements planning
business system, 6–7

C

CASE tools, 106
closed questions, 115, 120
communication
    defined, 113
    interviewing considerations,
    111–112
    nonverbal, 113
    with stakeholders, 32
    with users, 43
conflict resolution during workshops,
    102–103
constraints, 9
construction phase (BSLC), 4, 81–82
construction project life cycle, 50–51
consulted role (RACI model), 34–35
customer site visits, 112

D

deliverables
    assigning, 35–36
    determining strategies, 69–70
    project vs. product scope, 10
    scaling to projects, 26–29
deliver phase (BSLC), 4

design phase (BSLC), 4, 81–82
discovery sessions, 103, 107–108
documentation
    business requirements sample,
        139–160
    for ground rules, 43–44
    in SRLC, 4
    use cases sample, 161–183
    for user participation, 41–42
documentation reviews
    benefits, 125
    defined, 5
    in planning process, 20–23
    rules for, 125–126
    tailoring, 127

E

elicitation. *See* requirements
    elicitation
end-users. *See* users
Enterprise Analysis phase (BSLC),
    4, 20–23
evolutionary development model,
    52, 58–59, 66
eXtreme Programming (XP),
    105–106

F

functional vs. supplemental require-
    ments, 7–9
functions, in BRD, 11

G

government acquisition project life
    cycle, 50–51
ground rules, user, 43–44
guidelines as business rules, 8
guiding principles, 43–44

I

influence, stakeholder, 38–40

informed role (RACI model), 34–35
integrated project life cycle, 48
interface analysis/reviews
    benefits of, 129
    defined, 5, 129
    rules for, 129–130
    tailoring, 131
    types of meetings, 129–130
interviewing
    benefits of, 113
    communication challenges,
        111–112
    defined, 5, 111
    rules for, 115–117
    tailoring, 118
    tips for, 113–114
    types of, 112–113

J

JAD (joint application design),
    106–107
job shadowing, 112
joint application design (JAD),
    106–107

L

legacy maintenance model, 52,
    62–63, 66

M

methodology, 49
multiple build. *See* RAD (rapid
    application development) model

N

nonfunctional vs. functional require-
    ments, 7–9
nonverbal communication, 113

O

open-ended questions, 115, 120

Operations & Maintenance phase (BSLC), 4

P

personal interviews, 112
planning requirements activities. *See* requirements planning
planning teams, assembling, 19
Plutarch, 114
PMP (project management plan), 86–87
policies as business rules, 8
power, stakeholder, 38–40
procedures as business rules, 8
product life cycle, 48–49
product scope, 10
product vision document. *See* BRD (business requirements document)
products, 10
project complexity
   for interface analysis/reviews, 131
Project Complexity Model, 26–27
   scaling brainstorming, 100
   scaling interviews, 118
   scaling surveys, 123
   scaling workshop sessions, 110
   selecting project life cycle based on, 65–68
   for supplemental requirements, 135
   vee model, 52, 56–58
Project Complexity Model, 26–27
project life cycles
   agile development model, 52, 60–62, 66
   construction, 50–51
   defined, 49
   evolutionary development model, 52, 58–59, 66
   government acquisition, 50–51
   iterative nature of, 49
   legacy maintenance model, 52, 62–63, 66

prototyping model, 52, 63–66
purpose, 47–49
rapid application model, 52, 54–56, 66
selecting, 65–68
solution delivery strategies, 69–70
spiral development model, 52, 59–60, 66
tailoring, 68–69
training in, 70–71
variations in, 51–65
vee model, 52, 56–58, 66
waterfall model, 52–54, 66
project management plan (PMP), 86–87
project scope, 9–10
projects, 10, 26–29
prototyping model, 52, 63–66

Q

questions
   closed vs. open-ended, 115, 120
   in interviewing, 117
   in surveys, 121

R

RACI model, 34–36
RAD (rapid application development) model
   project life cycle of, 52, 54–56, 66
   workshop sessions, 106
regulations as business rules, 8
requirements analysis (SRLC)
   depicted, 4
   detailed plans, 78–79
   flow of information, 73–75
requirements documentation and validation (SRLC), 4, 73–75, 79–81
requirements elicitation (SRLC)
   brainstorming technique, 3, 32, 97–100

business solution life cycle, 4–6
defined, 1
detailed plans, 76–78
determining conclusion, 13–14
documentation reviews, 5, 20–23,
125–127
flow of information, 73–75
interface analysis/reviews, 5,
129–131
interviewing, 5, 111–118
planning for, 76–78
process overview, 91–95
sample task information, 85
supplemental requirements,
133–136
surveys, 5, 119–123
terminology, 6–13
workshop sessions, 101–110
requirements management plan.
See RMP (requirements management plan)
requirements phase (BSLC)
depicted, 4
detailed plans, 76–81
summary-level requirements plans,
81–82
workshop sessions, 101–110
requirements planning process.
See also project life cycles; RMP
(requirements management plan)
assembling teams, 19
assessing project components,
25–29
barriers, 83
flow of information into, 73–75
reviewing relevant documentation,
20–23
stakeholder analysis, 31–42
user analysis, 41–44
requirements specification (SRLC),
4, 79–80
responsible role (RACI model),
34–35

risk management
assessing project risk, 26–29
for interface analysis/reviews, 131
for interviews, 118
project life cycle selection and,
65–68
scaling brainstorming, 100
for stakeholder involvement, 32
for supplemental requirements,
135
with surveys, 123
in workshop sessions, 110
RMP (requirements management
plan)
approval needed, 87–88
barriers, 83
benefits of, 84–86
defined, 17, 83–84
detailed requirements phase plans,
76–81
elements of, 87
flow of information, 73–75
relationship to project
management plan, 86–87
sample plan, 185–202
summary-level requirements plans,
81–83
typical table of contents, 88
roles, stakeholder, 34–35

S

Scrum method, 106
Six Sigma technique, 104
solution development life cycle, 48
SOW (statement of work), 12–13
spiral development model, 52, 59–60,
66
SRLC (System Requirements Life
Cycle), 4
stakeholder analysis
purpose, 31–32
five-step process, 33–40
reexamining information, 40–41

stakeholders
  defined, 31–32
  identifying, 33–34
  identifying interest, 37–38
  identifying power and influence,
    38–40
  identifying roles, 34–36
  workshops involving, 102
statement of work (SOW), 12–13
supplemental requirements, 7–9,
    133–136
surveys
  benefits of, 120–121
  defined, 5, 119
  rules for, 121–122
  scaling, 123
  tailoring, 122
  types of, 120
System Requirements Life Cycle
    (SRLC), 4

T

tailoring
  brainstorming sessions, 100
  documentation reviews, 127
  interface analysis/reviews, 131
  interviews, 118
  project life cycles, 68–69
  supplemental requirements,
    134–135
  surveys, 122
  workshop sessions, 110
task analysis, 112–113
test phase (BSLC), 4, 81–82
training in project life cycles, 70–71

U

UML (Unified Modeling Language),
    105
use cases, 161–183
user analysis, 41–44

users
  communicating with, 43
  defined, 33
  elicitation process and, 93
  establishing ground rules with,
    43–44
  identifying, 41
  identifying champion, 43
  interface analysis/reviews,
    129–130
  justification for participation,
    41–42
  in workshop sessions, 109

V

vee model, 52, 56–58, 66
verbal communication. *See*
    communication

W

waterfall model, 52–54, 66
WBS (work breakdown structure),
    9–10, 76–77
workshop sessions
  agile requirements, 105–106
  business process improvement,
    104–105
  defined, 3, 101
  formal requirements, 104
  joint application design, 106–107
  rapid application design, 106
  requirements, 102–103
  rules for, 107–108
  tailoring, 110
  tips for, 108–109

X

XP (eXtreme Programming),
    105–106